Le   : how the timeless wisdom of one man can impact an entire generation

PRAISE FOR *LESSONS FROM A THIRD GRADE DROPOUT*

You will only have a few minutes to be in the presence of Rick Rigsby before you are deeply impacted by this wonderful man. His sense of humor, sense of purpose, and sense of place is immediately obvious, and before you're aware; you're drawn into his orbit, and you're on the ride of your life. At some point as you listen, you can't help but raise the question, either to yourself or to Rick: "Who's your Daddy?" You don't become the kind of person Dr. Rigsby has become without a significant voice in your life, and while there are many "voices" that have spoken into his life, there is one voice that rises above all of the others and of course this is the major thesis of the book. The template of success for the Rick Rigsby model is clearly described in this wonderful primer of life lessons. Passion is the result of an imprint upon one's life and Dr. Rigsby's passion for life and purpose is clearly the fruit of his father's example.

—Dr. Joseph L. Garlington,
Senior Pastor, Covenant Church of Pittsburgh,
Presiding Bishop, Reconciliation Ministries International

Dr. Rick Rigsby is a warm and compassionate human being who genuinely cares about other people. He also cares deeply about our country, and is concerned about the slippery slope we have been on as a society, with many of our traditional values deteriorating right before our eyes. He's on the front line, and he's out there making a difference. As one of the most powerful communicators I've ever seen, he has spoken to audiences all over the country, delivering an important message on why it's important to live honorably and do the right thing. And, people are paying attention! Dr. Rigsby was rated a top speaker, and received a standing ovation, at the 2006 National Character and Leadership Symposium at the United States Air Force Academy, for which I was personally responsible in organizing. Rick has now taken things to the next level and continued his important work by writing this wonderful book. It is chock full of practical wisdom and timeless lessons on how all of us can and should live our lives. I strongly endorse the many important messages in Rick's book. Furthermore, I highly suggest his book be read by parents, educators, coaches, young people, and anyone who genuinely cares about the future of our great country.

—Joseph W. Mazzola, Colonel, USAF (retired)
Former Director of the Center for Character Development
United States Air Force Academy

I love Rick Rigsby. My friend is a big man with a big heart who's learned a ton of life's hardest lessons. Here are some of the best wrapped up in unforgettable form.

—Dr. Stu Weber,
Bestselling Author and Speaker,
Senior Pastor, Good Shepherd Community Church,
Boring, Oregon

Dr. Rick Rigsby is spot on target with his new book that addresses the root issues of youth attitudes of the day. Providing advice and explanation to developing young people is strong medicine and will help educate them about the good of today's world with lessons from yesterday. *Lessons from a Third Grade Dropout* is a must read for today's young person.

—John M. Keever,
Vice President Marine Programs and Student Development,
California Maritime Academy
Commanding Officer, Training Ship Golden Bear

Many of us had dads that loved us enough during our growing up years to set a bar of character. Dads who worked hard, loved our families well and finished the race with honor. Rick and I both had those kinds of dads . . . and are thankful. If you did, your heart sings, if not, perhaps, you are ready to have a "dad" speak into your heart. My friend, Rick Rigsby, is just the kind of dad to speak into your spirit today. He has taken the message his father has carved in his heart and character and penned it in this book. My encouragement is to read it with a teachable heart, allow it to penetrate your soul and be willing to allow God to move in you to become the man God intends for you to be. Rick has the ability in his communication style to encourage, humor, stir and move you to conviction. If you are open to becoming the man of character God designed for you to become you are reading the right book. You will never be the same.

—Dr. Gary Rosberg,
President and Founder, America's Family Coaches,
Speaker, Author, Radio show co-host,
America's Family Coaches Live

Rick Rigsby has not only hit the nail on the head but he has driven the point all the way home. As only a man of integrity and character can. *Lessons from a Third Grade Dropout* has made me a better husband, father, coach and man. It should be required reading in all freshmen orientation classes. I will recommend it to all of our rookies before they get their careers started.

—Mike Clark
Strength and Conditioning Coach
Seattle Seahawks
2005 NFL Strength Coach of the Year

Rick Rigsby, with blunt honesty, pulls us into his experience dealing with pain and loss. He then levels the playing field by engaging his readers in a quest for wisdom that we each can join. He suggests and models looking to those who have "passed this way before" to gain insight. Rigsby, a skilled life coach, offers the challenge to move from making an impression to making an impact. His book merits not only a thoughtful read, but a renewed and enlarged commitment.

—Dr. Tom Fortson
President and CEO of Promise Keepers

Rick's ability to present a clear message using his personal life experiences enables everyone to understand and relate to him in a unique way. His ability to inspire and motivate go beyond the norm; he speaks about how companies can change to achieve more by going back to the basics of honesty, loyalty, trust, and character. He definitely made an impact when he came to visit us and everyone was very moved by what he had to say. His message still resonates as we try to make a difference in our business every day for our customers, partners and internal team members.

—Mark Pyatt
Director, Strategy and Cross-Industry Solutions
Global Industry Solution Marketing, SAP Labs, LLC

Rick Rigsby is one of the greatest communicators I know. In his book, *Lessons from a Third Grade Dropout,* he shares six powerful truths destined to make a lasting impact in the life of each reader. There's something special about Rick, his life and this message. I sincerely believe God's hand is on him to impact this generation with truths from a previous generation. Let these Lessons lift and lead you.

—John L. Mason
Speaker and Bestselling Author
An Enemy Called Average

As chaplain for the Texas A&M Football Team, Dr. Rick Rigsby has done an outstanding job with our young men. When he speaks, they listen . . . and they get the message!

—Charley F. North
Director of Football Operations
Texas A&M University

Dr. Rigsby has taken many of life's lessons and compiled them into a template for how to be successful in life, business and family. I was blessed with his knowledge and experience as a young man during my time at Texas A&M University. I was yearning for a voice of experience and knowledge and in search of a recipe for success. Dr. Rigsby directly impacted and influenced my work ethic and drive for success. The lessons learned during my college experience allowed me to accomplish a nine year NFL career. I was a kid from small town Texas who had big dreams, and through positive influence and hard work I have been able to exceed almost all of my own personal dreams. Take to heart the information in this book. Allow this wisdom to motivate you to accomplish your dreams. Rick Rigsby has had a profound impact on my life.

—Hunter Goodwin
Color Analyst, Fox Sports Southwest
Vice President, The Oldham Goodwin Group, LLC

Always a consistent message—one of hope, challenge, and growth—is what you will find in this moving book. Dr. Rick Rigsby practices the message that he shares, whether it be with his family, students, or acquaintances in all environments and situations. The words that you will read in *Lessons from a Third Grade Dropout* are the same as those that you would hear if you have the opportunity to interact with this wonderful individual. Dr. Rigsby is always one who leaves an impact.

—Mary R. Kane
Kansas FFA Association

During my years at Texas A&M, Dr. Rigsby used the lessons from his father's life to help me mature as a man. I held onto these lessons, not only during my collegiate years, but throughout my career in the NFL as well. Read this book. Learn from these lessons. They will have a profound impact on you as well.

—Bethel Johnson
Wide Receiver, New England Patriots

Rick is one of the most dynamic and inspiring individuals I have been associated with in my 25 years of experience in NCAA Division I athletics. I have personally seen how his heartfelt words of wisdom have significantly impacted the lives of hundreds of student-athletes over the years and have in turn inspired them to make a difference in their family, faith and community. Whether you are a coach, administrator or business professional, you'll appreciate these great life lessons that celebrate the values of a generation past and how they apply to our daily lives as we attempt to help shape the core values of our future leaders.

—Tim Cassidy
Associate Athletic Director, Football Operations
University of Nebraska

LESSONS
FROM A
THIRD GRADE
DROPOUT

LESSONS
FROM A
THIRD GRADE
DROPOUT

How the Timeless Wisdom of One Man
Can Impact an Entire Generation

RICK RIGSBY, Ph.D.

W Publishing Group

An Imprint of Thomas Nelson

Published in Nashville, Tennessee, by W Publishing, an imprint of Thomas Nelson.

Thomas Nelson titles may be purchased in bulk for educational, business, fund-raising, or sales promotional use. For information, please e-mail SpecialMarkets@ ThomasNelson.com.

Scripture quotations are taken from the New King James Version®. © 1982 by Thomas Nelson. Used by permission. All rights reserved.

Any Internet addresses, phone numbers, or company or product information printed in this book are offered as a resource and are not intended in any way to be or to imply an endorsement by Thomas Nelson, nor does Thomas Nelson vouch for the existence, content, or services of these sites, phone numbers, companies, or products beyond the life of this book.

ISBN 978-1-4041-0933-9 (jacketed hardcover)
ISBN 978-1-4041-0934-6 (eBook)

Library of Congress Cataloging-in-Publication Data

Rigsby, Rick, 1956–
Lessons from a third grade dropout / Rick Rigsby.
p. cm.
ISBN 10: 1-59951-000-6
ISBN 13: 978-1-59951-000-2
1. Conduct of life. 2. Kindness. I. Title.
BJ1531.R46 2006
170'.44—dc22
2006013643

Printed in the United States of America
18 19 20 21 22 LSC 10 9 8 7 6 5 4 3 2 1

To the loving memory of my parents
Roger Marion Rigsby and Viola Benjamin Rigsby
and
To Trina LaFaye Williams-Rigsby
Loving wife, caring mother, and adoring sister
Each of you finished the race so very well!

ACKNOWLEDGMENTS

A funny thing happened during a shopping trip to the Nordstrom's Rack, one of my wife's favorite vacation spots. While she was in sales heaven, I was figuring out if I'd have enough time to play a round of golf before the sun went down. We were attending a conference at the beautiful Fairmont Princess Hotel in Scottsdale, Arizona, which is adjacent to the TPC golf course—home of the Phoenix Open.

Right when my wife asked for the thirty-second time if *this blouse matched these pants*, I discovered an escape plan! I spotted a guy that looked very familiar and headed his direction. He had just spoken at the conference we were attending. When I walked up to John Mason, I had no idea he was a bestselling author and successful publisher. I really had no idea that one day he would become *my* publisher, and one of my dearest friends. My goal was to compliment a speaker on a job well done. The chance meeting resulted in an hour conversation. By the time we said our good-byes, our wives had become instant friends, and John had convinced me that this "Third-Grade Dropout" was a story worth telling. It was an hour that would change my life.

John, words cannot express the love and admiration I have for you. Your steadfast belief in this project and in me came at just the right time. You have got to be the best manuscript "coach" in the country. Your firm, though delicate, handling of each draft encouraged and challenged me to communicate a message rather than merely write a book. You are not just my publisher. You and Linda are among our dearest friends!

And to your amazing Thomas Nelson staff in Tulsa, a huge thank you for all your assistance—especially to Michelle Mason for your godly encouragement and to Denise Benson for never losing your patience—regardless of how many times I called!

We were concerned that the Thomas Nelson Marketing Department in Nashville may have difficulty promoting an unknown author. I would like to thank Jennifer Deshler and her remarkable staff for alleviating any concern, and for believing in this project and working endlessly to promote *Lessons from a Third Grade Dropout.*

My greatest appreciation is extended to the entire

Thomas Nelson Publishing family. What an honor to be affiliated with an organization that epitomizes godly integrity and world-class excellence. I consider it a high privilege to represent you.

I am especially thankful to my editor, Ramona Richards. Thank you for carefully cultivating the very best way to capture and communicate the lessons from my dad. You're an awesome wordsmith . . . and a very kind person!

The thought of writing a book actually never occurred to me until Steve Farrar gave me the opportunity of a lifetime—a chance to speak to several thousand men during one of his awesome weekend conferences. After my presentation, Steve said, "Rick, you need to write a book." Thank you, Steve, for your friendship, but also for seeing what I was not able to. Thank you for encouraging men everywhere to *Finish Strong!*

Also speaking at the Farrar conference that particular weekend were Stu Weber and Gary Rosberg. Stu, I always will covet your wisdom and encouragement. You are the epitome of a *Tender Warrior*!

Gary, words cannot express my love and admiration for you. From our very first meeting, you have supported me in every venture, and in the process have become one of my very best friends. You have set the standard for families in America not just with your acclaimed national radio show—but more importantly with your life, the way you love your family, and the way you practice what you preach. Yes, my friend, I will *guard my heart!*

I am a firm believer in the African proverb that, "it takes an entire village to raise a child." My village has extended throughout the United States and includes some of the finest mentors in the world. Among them are: Ben and Flo Anderson, Steve Brydon, Vince and Melanie Bloom, John Cagle, Gary Collier, Kay Conlee, Shirl and Jack DeBay, Dwight Edwards, Flip and Susan Flippen, David Frank, Sonja Foss, Philmore Graham, Noreen Johnson, Steve Kragthorpe, Dominic LaRusso, Charley Leistner, Wes Matthews, Marty Medhurst, Steve Morris, Al and Della Nichols, Dennis Patrick, Bobby Glenn Powell, Linda Putnam, Mark Pyatt, Kurt Ritter, Ken Rucker, Doris and Ray Sanders, Rev. Ray Shelton, Rev. Terry Teykl, LeMar Treadwell, Benjamin Williams, Randy Wimpee, and Rev. Roger Witlow. Each of you have had a profound impact on my life.

A very special thanks to that first village—the elders who lived on the 1100 block of Louisiana Street in Vallejo, California: Aunt Audrey and Uncle Fay Thompson, the Browns, the Johnsons, the Hollins, the Pools, the Lindsays, the Whitesides, the Wilsons, Mr. Stevenson, Mr. Blair, Jesse, and Dave.

To my spiritual father in the faith, Bishop Joseph

Garlington, to and my brothers and sisters at Reconciliation Ministries International. Thank you, Dad and Pastor Barbara (Mom), for setting the standard. It's not just how you preach but how you live. Janet and I are forever grateful for being part of the "cluster!"

I am honored to be in covenant relationship with a band of accountability brothers who are mighty men of God. They are: Mike Clark, Gary Drews, Todd Ewalt, Clarence Grant, Paul Holderfield, Jr., Frank Koons, John Mason, Patrick McKinney, Pierre Moranza, Ron Moser, Jeff Paine, J. J. Ramirez, Gary Rosberg, Calvin Wheeler, Gordon Wong, Frank Krug and my best friend, Haywood Robinson. Men, let us commit to God and each other to stay clean and finish strong!

Trying to juggle a university schedule with over 200 engagements can be a challenge. Now add a two-year commitment to write a book on top of that, and you better have a good support team. I have the best. To my staff at Rick Rigsby Communications, a mere thank you does not seem sufficient. So how about one of Janet's carrot cakes at every staff meeting for the next year? With sincere gratitude and a heart of thanksgiving, I am earnestly indebted to Cynthia Forman-Haynes, Brenda Kibble, Megan Roth, Megan Neveu, Callie Macfarlan, Bess Cave, Michelle Enriquez, Jayme Dobbins, and our Vice President, Janet Rigsby.

ACKNOWLEDGMENTS

When scheduling conflicts do not allow me to attend an event, Dr. Ben Welch willingly accommodates with such excellence and excitement that people often forget they invited me! Thank you, Ben. You're a dear friend and a brilliant communicator! A very a special thank you is extended to our "creative geniuses" and part-time roadies, Aaron Cave and Shaun Menary. May God continue to prosper RandomShirts.com and allow you to bless other ministries as you have ours. You guys are incredible! Finally, my appreciation is offered to Dolly Havens for her hours of editorial support that assisted in the completion of this manuscript.

To the Prayer Team that supports Rick Rigsby Ministries. You are the power plant! For all the countless hours behind the scenes, nothing would be possible without your intercession. Specifically, I wish to thank: Rev. Evan and Nancy Henderson, Kenny and Kathy Johnson, Frank and Karla Koons, Elaine Krol, Barbara McCulloch, Ray and Doris Sanders, Daryl and Rosie Talley, Ted and Delores Wyatt and our coordinators, Al and Della Nichols. And thanks to a special woman and dear friend, Muriel Turner of Chico, California, who decades ago prophesied that a young news reporter would someday leave television and enter the ministry—long before a ministry was ever conceived.

A very special thanks to our dear friends, Chris,

Kimberly, Koa, and Charles Dey. Your family has become our family. Your "island paradise" has become our second home—and a perfect setting for writing books! Thank you for sharing your life with us.

I always will be indebted to former Texas A&M head football coach R.C. Slocum. It was during my tenure on his staff as Life Skills Coordinator that he gave me freedom to develop and teach our football players *Lessons from a Third Grade Dropout*. Coach Slocum, you're in the Texas Sports Hall of Fame because you're a great coach. But I think your greatest accomplishment is that you always placed character before wins and losses.

To my brother Bobby, the other primary beneficiary of my Dad's teachings. We enjoyed the best childhood imaginable. Although we thought our parents were too strict, we never doubted their love for and belief in us. Bobby, I am so proud of you. And I know Mom and Dad are in heaven just gleaming over their son—the Honorable Robert Ray Rigsby, Superior Court Judge, Washington, D.C.

When constructing the early years of my father's life and impact, I leaned heavily on Rigsby family members— particularly my dad's surviving siblings. To Olin Rigsby, Opal Rigsby-Mills, and Edward Rigsby, thank you for the hours of conversations you allowed me to record. I will treasure for a lifetime all the stories I did not know about how kind and respectful and determined my father was. I thank God for the three of you and the impact you have had on my life. Do know that the wisdom from your generation will continue!

I am overwhelmed with unspeakable joy to call four children my sons. To Jeremiah and Andrew, I am so glad you got a few years with "Paw Paw." You both have acquired some of his traits. Zachary and Joshua, by the time you came along, your grandpa was in heaven, but you still managed to get the genes!

I see my dad in all four of you—and it pleases me beyond measure. Jeremiah Benjamin Rigsby, you have your grandfather's charm and class. Andrew David Rigsby, you possess Paw Paw's wisdom and courage. Zachary Benton Rigsby, you have your granddaddy's tender heart. You are so kind! Joshua Wellington Rigsby—Pup, your wit reflects the essence of Roger Rigsby in every way! Guard your hearts, tender warriors, and finish strong!

A decade ago, I thought my life was over. That's the feeling in your gut when you look into the casket of your spouse. But God had a different plan. He sent me an angel named Janet Butcher.

To my darling sweetheart Janet, thank you for rescuing me. It's not easy to love a widower. But with amazing grace and tender compassion you have loved me back from the depths of hell and helped me to see the purpose that God has for my life. Almost from the moment we met, you have breathed life into this writing project. While I get the credit for writing the book, I wish to acknowledge that for the last seven years—five years before a book deal—you prayed over me that the wisdom of my dad would surface clearly and purposefully on each page. Thank you, Janet, for sharing stunning sunsets and star-filled nights! What a daily joy it is to fall in love with you all over again!

FOREWORD

I am so proud that Dr. Rick Rigsby has finally compiled the wonderful gems of wisdom that he has shared with my players, my coaches, and me, as well as audiences all over the world.

I first met Rick on an airplane in 1994 and was immediately struck by his sincerity and wisdom, and felt that he could have a great "impact" on my team. At that time, I had a growing concern that we were not doing all we could do as coaches to influence the lives of the young men in our program. We sent our players to class and taught them the fundamentals of math, English, science, and history, etc. On the football field, we taught them the fundamentals of blocking, tackling, keeping their pads down, etc. My concern was that we did not have a good plan to teach them the real skills one needs to live life—those essential "life skills" that lead to a productive, happy life.

At the time, I had never heard those words used together. Now, you hear that term frequently. I shared with Rick my burden to do more than teach academics and football and asked for his thoughts on this subject. He understood exactly what I was talking about and began immediately to relate some of the lessons he had learned from his father. The flight we were on was too quickly over, but we agreed to get together at the earliest opportunity to discuss this idea further. After several meetings, Dr. Rick Rigsby agreed to accept the position that I created for him as Life Skills Coordinator.

That was a great day for everyone involved with our program at Texas A&M. From that time, Rick was totally involved in everything that we did. He created a syllabus for a course in life skills, based on the Lessons that he had learned from a third grade dropout. He taught that course to all of our players. He led devotions with the team and staff and helped all of us with our own Life Skills. While going through the tragic loss of his wife, Trina, to cancer, I witnessed as Rick demonstrated his understanding of the Lessons. Dr. Rick Rigsby has lived a lot of life and has a great understanding of the tools that one, of any age, needs to be a winner at the game of life. *Lessons from a Third Grade Dropout* will be a powerful resource for everyone who reads it.

> R.C. Slocum
> Former Head Football Coach, Texas
> A&M University
> Member, Texas Sports Hall of Fame

CONTENTS

PREFACE

As I turned in the final draft of this manuscript to my publisher, I came across an article in *USA Today* that astounded me. The article was titled, "Dropouts say their schools expected too little of them" (*USA Today*, 3/2/06, p. 9D). Reporter Greg Toppo noted that the survey—sponsored by the Bill and Melinda Gates Foundation—reveals that "nearly two-thirds (of high school dropouts) say they would have worked harder if expectations had been higher."

The survey points to a critical problem in society today. We live in an era of low expectations. In fact, we tend to celebrate low expectations. Our goal is to do whatever it takes just to get by. Just get the job done—that's our rallying cry. And the most critical component to our getting by is to look good in the process!

The way in which we choose to live and work today is

a far cry from the purposeful living of our parents. I recall the elders of an earlier era telling me that the bar of excellence is lowered with each passing generation. At age ten, I thought—what a stupid statement. At age fifty, I think—what an absolute truth. Have we reached the point in our society where it is more important to look good rather than be good? Has the pride in doing good work been replaced by self-entitlement, perfect offices, and slick suits?

The purpose of this book is to re-acquaint readers with the wisdom—the common sense that was practiced simply and unwittingly by those who represent a generation gone by. This was an era of individuals who worked hard without complaining. They committed to doing whatever was necessary to help the company and support their families. They took pride in doing a good job. They worked without ceasing. And they maintained high standards—they had *high expectations* for themselves and the others they were responsible for.

One such member of this generation was a third-grade dropout. Yet, his lack of a formal education pales in comparison to the impact one life can make. This man never ever hid behind an excuse. He never allowed his problems to determine his present or affect his future. He realized that destiny was a choice and not a chance. And in living his simple way, the profoundness of his life is impacting a new generation today.

This book communicates some of the lessons from that man's life. It's the kind of wisdom that is rare in society today. It's the kind of wisdom that will cause you to be a better person, a greater leader, a more effective worker. It's the kind of wisdom that will cause you to make an impact . . . rather than just an impression.

That man is my father, and this book contains the story of how a life can be enhanced . . . a corporate culture changed . . . a family united . . . by living the simple lessons of a third-grade dropout.

CHAPTER 1

WHAT'S WRONG WITH HOW WE LIVE?

GOING THROUGH THE MOTIONS

Losing a spouse is the worst thing that ever happened to me. Staring into the casket, which held my wife's body, was like looking into a deep, dark hole. I was lost. No direction. No future. No hope.

For my two young sons and me, our lives as we knew them were over. Jeremiah and Andrew missed Mommy, and there was no way to hide the harsh and sudden reality that she would never be with us on another picnic, never decorate another Christmas tree, never sip hot cocoa around a campfire, and never cheer during a T-Ball game.

Never is such a definitive word. Never. It's the stuff death produces. It's hard to breathe within the space created by never. At some point you have to make a choice. Am I going to live or am I going to die? Am I going to find the faith and the courage to pick myself up and try to live again, or am I going to merely exist?

At forty-one years of age, I had to ask myself, *will I be satisfied spending the rest of my life going through the motions?* At least for the moment, going through the motions looked very appealing.

Going through the motions—what I refer to as just making an impression—is an easy task. It's like going through life only satisfying the basic minimum requirements. No one questions your motives, little is expected of you, there really is no great pressure to improve, and most of all, little if anything in your life has to change.

I was a widower. People felt too much sorrow to hold me accountable. I answered to very few people. Merely "existing" comforted me. To exist offers the illusion of freedom without any responsibility. Our present culture encourages effortless living since all that matters is appearing successful.

In a real sense, I was dying a slow death. I had no desire whatsoever to venture beyond the realm of perception, and after a while, perception did not matter. But that's fine in a world that requires little else.

Impressionistic living is tolerated with exceptional ease especially if you understand the power of the visual image. The logic is simple. Ours is a visual world with citizens who delight in those who *appear good or gifted or great*. Thus, we find it pleasantly acceptable for morality to be replaced by materialism, principle by popularity, or character by convenience. If one can polish an image or dress to create a certain kind of appearance, then success is within reach. Friends, possessions, and surroundings have value inasmuch as they are significant metaphors used in the construction of an image that promises temporal rewards and immediate gratification.

As we examine our present landscape, the prevailing wisdom is undeniably clear: *you don't have to lose a spouse to merely exist.* In fact, you do not even have to encounter difficult times. With pretty friends and the right stuff, you can build the perception of excellence and success. Making a good impression costs little. Best of all, one need not venture through life's difficult waters to seek strength or revelation. After all, who would choose difficulty if it's not required for personal development? I certainly would not. And I am not alone.

A prevailing paradigm in our culture permeates the minds of citizens who see no reason to make a change for the better. It's a refusal to accurately assess, analyze, and adapt to one's present environment. In other words, most of us are in denial. I know I was once. I used to weigh 404 pounds, but I told myself that I

> FRIENDS, POSSESSIONS, AND SURROUNDINGS HAVE VALUE INASMUCH AS THEY ARE SIGNIFICANT METAPHORS USED IN THE CONSTRUCTION OF AN IMAGE THAT PROMISES TEMPORAL REWARDS AND IMMEDIATE GRATIFICATION.

was not—in the words of my doctor—*morbidly obese*. I knew I was simply a "big man."

I know . . . "denial." The person who weighs 300 pounds is morbidly obese. Now, at half the weight I once was, I see clearly that the issue was not weight. With the help of my physician and best friend, Haywood Robinson, M.D., we mapped out a life plan that incorporated a healthy lifestyle as opposed to occasional dieting.

In my case, obesity was the result of rebellion brought on by denial! The very same denial which threatened my life and obstructed my view of the real issue functions similarly in our culture today. We don't really see a need to change. As long as we're happy, fed, clothed, and most of all appear successful, why would we desire any modification?

So, why should I do more than the basic minimum required? Following Trina's funeral, I found it more convenient to offer the appearance that everything was fine. I would answer "fine" to inquiries from family and friends. I taught classes and things were "fine" with my students. Even at the place where death created devastation, I tried to make our home feel "fine" as friends assisted in everything from helping with carpooling to trimming the Christmas tree. How long could I pull off this act? How long could I convince others and myself that there was really no need for change? I went into a trance. I went through the motions. I choreographed each mediocre step and scripted every predictable response. I could have lived like this forever.

What is so despicable about a life like this? What is the big deal? And, why should anyone care? If a pastor or priest wishes to exist and coast for a while, what's the great sin? If a coach loses that competitive edge and chooses to go through the motions, what's the great loss? If a college student decides to fake out parents and professors while wasting four years and thousands of dollars, what's the big failure? If the head of a corporation has no compassion for employees, yet wears Armani, drives a Jaguar, and travels between vacation homes while the wages of company workers are frozen, is that such a great travesty? *What's so wrong with how we live?*

I would not have survived losing my wife without my faith, my family, and my friends. However, it took more than prayer and fellowship to deliver me from the paralysis brought on by going through the motions. You may find yourself in a similar situation. You may be in a relationship that frustrates you more with each passing day. Or you may be in a situation you have labeled as hopeless. Family and friends help to a point. But you are well aware that it's going to take a miracle before your life returns to something that resembles normal.

As a child I learned the biblical truth that *faith without works is dead.* I had to go to work. And not to a new job or in a new career. I had to work on a new mindset. I had to change my paradigm. I had to move from pity to passion, from grief to gratitude. I had to shift from going through the motions to living above my circumstances. In essence, I had to move from making an impression to making an impact.

As I pondered how to make such a radical shift in my thinking, I reflected on wise words deposited in my heart over the years by my parents. Like many others, I have found it amazing that the older I get, the wiser my parents become! I would ask myself, "OK, what would Mother do if suddenly her passion for living vanished? How would Daddy react if the love of his life passed away?" I continued asking, "How would they respond to a broken heart?" My parents were like so many others from a generation that reflected such practical wisdom. I just knew if I would quiet myself and listen, their words would return to my heart and help lead me out of my misery.

The lack of wisdom in our present society poses a critical threat to the quality of our lives. A substantial disconnect exists in our world today which results in a massive division between generations. The division does not interrupt economic, social, or even political channels. It's a divide that separates one generation from the wisdom of an earlier era. At stake is the loss of a society's greatest resource. We're not talking natural resources. Technology and innovation can overcome our most primitive efforts to mine coal or extract gold. The resource I speak of is the ultimate gift we receive from those who have ventured before us. That resource is wisdom—something our folks referred to as "common sense."

Simply stated, the great disconnect is between an older generation of *doers* verses a contemporary generation of *viewers*. Tom Brokaw discusses the former generation in his excellent book, *The Greatest Generation*. Brokaw describes the citizens of this era as those who survived the Great Depression, fought to protect our homeland during World War II, rebuilt the infrastructure of a post-war America, planted seeds that would eventually produce the greatest technological revolution in the history of humankind, and launched the greatest baby boom in history.

You may know some who represent this generation. They are remarkable in their simple yet profound work ethic. They represent an era of people who valued their work and took pride in doing a good job. They were hard-working, decent people who arrived early to the job, did not run from responsibility, and gave maximum effort.

Their work habits were not for show. Doing a good job simply was a way of life.

One representative of this generation is Roger Marion Rigsby, a third-grade dropout, yet the wisest man I have ever met. And I got the chance to spend a lot of time with him, learn from him, and follow his model. Roger Rigsby was not merely my mentor. He was my father.

Reared in Huntsville, Texas during the early part of the twentieth century, my dad was forced to leave elementary school to help work on the family farm. His brother Edward says that life was tough and money was scarce for African-American families in this small community nestled on the border of the Piney Woods of East Texas. Sharecropping was commonplace, and to survive, families farmed, ranched, hunted, and did whatever was necessary to put bread on the table. Supporting a large family during the lean years of post-depression America offered little in the areas of comfort and luxury. You did what was required. And you did it to the best of your ability.

Roger Rigsby grew up in a large family. Grandpa Rufus was a hard worker who provided for his family and commanded respect from local townspeople. He challenged his children to live similar lives. Grandma—affectionately known as Mamo—was a God-fearing woman with a strong resolve and even stronger faith. Their children—Olin, Vivian, Roger, Miriam, Opal, Edward, and Macy learned valuable lessons from difficult times, and they deposited those nuggets into the lives of the next generation of Rigsbys.

My father's surviving siblings (Olin, Edward, and Opal) note that even at an early age, they could see something different about my dad. His steadfast work ethic was paralleled only by his sense of justice. He respected all people, feared no man, and was kind to a fault. Such traits are quite admirable for anyone, and especially for a person of color trying to survive in a society where segregation was the framework of life. The countless stories from my father's childhood and early adult years—including a tour of duty in the Army during World War II—construct a clear and convincing parallel between the hardships endured and the values forged in his life that eventually would impact an entire generation of baby boomers.

Learning from the wisdom of an earlier generation may very well be the societal glue that reconnects our society with the traits and values of an era that practiced common sense values as a lifestyle.

An interruption in the flow of wisdom will not necessarily threaten technological supremacy. Few eras have witnessed the technology boom of the twentieth century. However, an interruption in the transfer of wisdom produces an invisible malaise just as destructive as sickness, war, and famine. A culture whose leaders neglect to model wisdom produces teams and organizations in a similar manner. The outcome is a society in great peril—a society that seeks simple solutions for complex problems. Such a society is satisfied with mediocrity as long as workers put in eight hours. The environment produces workers who emphasize appearance over substance, personality over principle, and convenience over character. What good is technological supremacy without authentic leadership? What good is an information superhighway without trust-worthy travelers?

Howard Hendricks, distinguished professor at Dallas Theological Seminary, cites the major problem in leader-ship today as a lack of character among leaders. Sadly, though accurately, Hendricks' observation enjoys sub-stantial evidence. Our lack of character is not cloaked in political affiliation, ethnic wardrobe, or economic status. The lack of integrity appears boundless—ravaging the ranks of corporations, the political arena, service orga-nizations, schools, government, and religious institutions. What once was considered unthinkable conduct among priests is now commonplace. Coaches being indicted and corporate moguls going to jail are common news today.

I was privileged recently to have lunch with Dr. Hendricks, affectionately known by thousands of admiring former DTS students as "Prof." His admon-ishment to me was not to be a good preacher or a good writer, but to be a good person who stays clean and finishes strong. Prof was saying in his own way, "Rick, always place character above gifting." It was a one-hour lunch that will stay with me for a lifetime.

The great disconnect of the new millennium separates two generations at its most fundamental juncture. The grave concern is not whether America will lose her dominance as a global leader or superpower. The major issue facing business, organizations, institutions, and schools in the new century is whether we are willing to undergo a major paradigm shift that reconstitutes our priorities. America is at a crossroads and faces many great challenges.

> **WHAT GOOD IS TECHNOLOGICAL SUPREMACY WITHOUT AUTHENTIC LEADERSHIP? WHAT GOOD IS AN INFORMATION SUPERHIGHWAY WITHOUT TRUSTWORTHY TRAVELERS?**

I argue that this crossroads is the alluring yet deceitful choice of either going through the motions or adopting the deliberate, life-altering manifesto that suggests a stronger family, a stronger community, and a stronger work environment by citizens demonstrating an individual commitment to make an impact. Suspended in the balance are present business practices and future generations of young people with a galaxy of ideas, ingenuity, and creativity to change our world. But without a determined commitment to be a decent, hard-working, and honest human being, how strong can a superpower be? How successful can a corporation become? What kind of legacy will a coach leave? How will a leader be able to inspire others?

The mission of this book is convincing our present generation to re-learn some timeless lessons. We must reconnect our generation's leaders, workers, families, and children to a few core values from an earlier era. A growing number of individuals have found that the values we were forced to consume with our TV dinners and Jiffy Pop Popcorn are not as barbaric and archaic and restrictive as childhood might have us believe. As we dust the age off a few of these time-tested beliefs, we may find answers to many of today's problems.

Clearly, the previous generation fell short in many areas, most notably race relations and gender inequalities. While not condoning such pejorative offenses, my goal here is to highlight and celebrate a few of the values that sustained a nation through war, famine, and despair.

As I work on this portion of the book, I am surrounded by a gentle breeze off the South Pacific waters surrounding the Hawaiian Islands. When you're here, the horrific reminders of Pearl Harbor are not far away. I think about the maturity and courage it took for yesterday's citizens to not only fight, but also rebuild from the ruins of a world war. There was something special in the core of those individuals—male and female. They produced something of value that compelled one to do the right thing and embedded it in the culture of a corporation, in the texture of a team, and in the fabric of a family. There was something very noble about a young soldier who dared to give his life for the sake of his country. Gratefully, we witness the same valiant sacrifices on the battlefield today. Regrettably, few are the other venues where similar heroics fill the landscape.

There is a stark contrast when you compare yesterday's workers with the images of our citizens today who cheat and steal and are carted off to prison in a seemingly never-ending parade. There is a startling void in our leadership today. It is a void produced by everyday citizens who do not take pride in what they do, would rather finish first than do things right, and would rather look good than be good. Our goal in the new millennium is *to make a good impression.*

What were those values that embedded that culture? What caused a person to put in an honest day's work without examining the clock every thirty minutes? What cultural components reinforced a code of conduct among employees that forbade so many of the infractions prevalent today? What caused a man to tell the truth or a woman to do the right thing? What produced in people a willingness to help others, to look out for others, to genuinely care for others? In the past fifty years, our world has produced technical giants and moral midgets. Such a dichotomy cannot sustain progress of any type, no matter how great. And it is this ethical paradox that begs the question, "what's wrong with how we live?"

Roger Rigsby lived a very simple yet profound life. As a child growing up in the San Francisco Bay Area community of Vallejo, I really did not think much about my father. He was like all the dads of his era—tough on his children!

Dad had a no-nonsense approach to life. He knew how to have fun, but would never allow himself to become carried away in the moment. Maybe it was his upbringing, his military training, or his own code of personal discipline. Whatever it was, my father was always in control, always at his best, always doing the right thing, and always helping others.

Dad—just like his father—demanded the same for my brother and me. He was tough, but fair. Dad did not tolerate a lot of excuses either! If he told you to do something, it had better be done. Period. How imaginative my college students have become over the years with their excuses as to why a paper is not turned in or why they did so poorly on an exam. I think about my contemporaries and all the excuses we make for not getting the job done. I just have to smile as I am reminded of a man who would turn a deaf ear to excuses. They simply did not fly with Roger Rigsby.

How would your life change if you stopped excusing yourself so often? How would the quality of your life improve if you kept your word, did what you said you would do, and held yourself more accountable in the process? My father held a high standard, kept his word, and expected his sons to do likewise.

I recall one evening when my father had cooked supper while Mother was asleep before her graveyard shift at the local hospital. Like most ten-year-olds, I suddenly and mysteriously developed a strong dislike for a particular food my father had prepared. This night it was baked cod. I told my father in no uncertain terms that I did not like it and would not eat it. My father's response was simple, uncomplicated, and not given to exaggeration, "Ricky, you will not leave this table until you eat the fish." Dad gave his order at six o'clock. I sat at the table as my father retired for the evening in front of the television. I was determined not to eat the fish. Around ten o'clock that evening, I finally discovered the nerve to leave the kitchen table, walk to the TV room, and ask my father if I had to continue sitting. He asked if I had eaten the fish. I responded that I had taken a few bites. I immediately was released from "kitchen table prison."

The point here is that my father was not wishy-washy.

He was not one who minced words. And he certainly did not go back on his word. If he said it, he meant it. And if he said he was going to do something, he did it. Right or wrong. Popular or unpopular.

Are there people in your life who are solid as a rock? Do they *say what they mean and mean what they say?* Although it's rare to find a person like this today, they still exist. And I guarantee, they are the kind of people you want to hire. They are the type of people you want to fill your company with. They are the type of employee you want representing you at the trade show or in the boardroom. This is the type of physician you want. This is the kind of teacher you admire. These are citizens you can trust. These are people you can depend on. These are the students who finish assignments on time. These are the employees who work extra hours to get the job completed. These are the kind of persons who make great leaders because of one major reason. They have integrity; there is a consistency between what they say and what they do. Integrity was Roger Marion Rigsby.

As I stood in front of my wife's casket that horrible September afternoon, I did not stand alone. My sons and I were flanked by supportive family members and sympathetic friends. However, one person stood taller than all others. Dad was there during the worst times of my life and the best. He was there that bleak fall afternoon saying very little in his customarily reserved manner. Yet measuring his simple yet profound words like a Winston Churchill disciple, he offered both comfort and compassion, and as it turned out, one final lesson. This book is about that man, and the lessons I learned from that third-grade dropout.

CHAPTER 2

KIND DEEDS ARE
NEVER LOST

A CHOICE TO BE KIND

In the movie, *Mr. Saturday Night,* Billy Crystal turns in a marvelous performance as Buddy Young, Jr., a budding Jewish comedian who has no rival. Buddy can make a snake laugh. Crystal's fictional character begins in the living room after a typical Sunday family dinner. He and his brother Stan entertain Mom, Uncle Moe, and all the family. Success in a local talent show opens the door to clubs and dinner halls and eventually network television. With Stan managing his career, Buddy Young, Jr.— dubbed *Mr. Saturday Night*—is on his way to fulfilling his childhood dream of being the greatest comedian ever. There's just one small problem. Buddy Young, Jr. is not a kind man.

He perfected rudeness into an art form. And it is his lack of kindness that eventually turns his dream into a nightmare. Buddy never enjoys the prominence of being a major star. In fact, his latter years find him pathetic— estranged in relationships and talented at burning bridges and condemning people. What once began as a promising career ends sadly decades later with Buddy still on the road and carrying his own bags. Instead of network TV, cruise ships, and the Poconos, a tired, lonely, and bitter old man performs for handfuls at senior centers and condominium recreation rooms.

Is the lack of kindness killing your career? Does your lack of kindness affect relationships? Are you stuck in the basement of life? Has your rise to the top stalled? Are you passed over constantly when it comes to promotions? Are you finding yourself less than satisfied despite your position in the organization? Are you unfulfilled in your present position? Have you discovered that status and sleek business cards fail to comfort feelings of inadequacy and insecurity? Do you find yourself just going through the motions? Are you merely stuck in neutral? Or, worse yet, in reverse? Are you watching others live your dreams? Are you making a choice to allow your season to pass you by? In your heart you know that receiving more training is not the answer. Developing additional skill sets of technological competency is not what is needed. You can receive the best training available, possess all the skill in the world, and own a wealth of knowledge, but still have a resume stamped "incomplete" or a life labeled "unsatisfied" or a dream marked "unfulfilled." I have great news! Your noble quest toward living a complete, enriched life begins simply and unwittingly with a choice to be kind.

KIND DEEDS ARE NEVER LOST

My brother and I must have heard this phrase a thousand times growing up. Our dad did not have many rules nor did he speak many words. So when he would repeat something daily, monthly, or year after year we figured it was important. Dad would share this phrase throughout the day and each night when the time came to share a Bible verse before dinner. For my entire life—the entire forty-plus years that I knew my Dad—before every meal, he would recite the words, "Kind deeds are never lost" (see Rom. 2:6–7).

The impact of his words is emotional as I reflect on how deeply this man valued kindness. To Dad, kindness was not just a word. Kindness was a way of life. Edward Rigsby, my Dad's youngest brother put it this way:

Roger always went out of his way to be the kindest among us. Even as children, there seemed to be a difference about him—a kindness rare among all the other boys and girls. As a man, he was the symbol of kindness. He always placed family and friends before himself. His family was more important than anything on Earth; my brother was among the kindest. His life impacts and influences me to this very day.

Uncle Edward, affectionately known as "Baby Ray," went on to earn a bachelor's and a master's degree, taught school, was a vice principal, coached football, and had a remarkable career serving several schools in the greater Houston area. Baby Ray said among his greatest inspirations was his brother, Roger Rigsby.

My father's sister, my Aunt Opal, also speaks of her brother's kindness. Aunt Opal could not stop talking about how kind Roger was:

> Ricky, your father (Roger) was such a kind and sweet man. Even as a child, I always could depend on my brother to do the right thing and to treat me with kindness. He was kind to our entire family. There are just not many people on this earth who are as kind as your daddy.

My father's kindness was a motivating force in those who observed his life. How different would your life look if you were more kind today? How different would your marriage look if you chose kindness over rudeness? What effect would more kindness in front of employees and colleagues have on your leadership? In essence, how would more kindness in your life influence those around you?

THE POSITIVE POWER OF KINDNESS

How does kindness enhance one's life? Before we can talk about how kindness impacts a culture, let's discuss the individual influence kindness has on the heart and soul of a person. If you are kind to others, expect the law of reciprocity to be active in your life. The more you give away, the more you receive. My father—with a third-grade education—understood the law of reciprocity. "Son, kind deeds are never lost." Your acts of kindness are stored in the vaults of the soul. The kinder you are, the more fulfilling your life will be. The Bible says it is better to give than to receive—something rarely on display in our world today. However, you show me a person who practices giving as a lifestyle, and I'll show you a wealthy person.

A powerful example comes from the life of Chick-fil-A® restaurant founder Truett Cathy. Cathy took a simple chicken sandwich and turned it into a company reporting sales of approximately $800 million per year. In Jim Braham's article, "The Spiritual Side," Braham discusses how godly principles help CEOs in business. Braham discovered that kindness and giving are both at the heart of Truett Cathy's success:

> Cathy, who with his wife Jeannette recently celebrated their fiftieth anniversary, remains active not only with

his company, but with his many volunteer and philanthropic activities. For the last 45 years, he has taught Sunday School for 13-year-old boys. And through his company's 11 foster-care homes, more than 100 children from disadvantaged or troubled backgrounds are getting a better start in life. "The greatest joys of living are the joys of giving," Cathy says. "Seeing these kids grow up and be somebody is an experience you just can't buy with dollars and cents."[1]

Although he possessed little in terms of material possessions, my father was a wealthy man. I believe it was because of a lifetime bestowing kind acts upon people. I recall a story told at my father's funeral by our former pastor at Good Samaritan Missionary Baptist Church in Vallejo, California. Rev. Calvin Miller noted a time when a family emergency required him to make a cross-country trip. My father gave the pastor his gasoline credit card—no strings attached. Rev. Miller told the story at my father's funeral. As I listened, I recall thinking, "That's my Dad!" His philosophy was you don't give based on what you have or what you don't have. You give when there is a need. We had little to nothing. But in an act of unselfish kindness, my father gave everything he had to help someone else.

Maybe the answer to your most pressing need or

opportunity is wrapped up in a kind deed you can do. Maybe a chance to be kind is just the key that unlocks the door to greater opportunity!

You may not have had a mother or father who practiced kindness. Perhaps you need a little help learning how to be kind. Did you know there is a website designed for the sole purpose of encouraging people toward kindness and helping them to locate opportunities to be kind in their communities? The Random Acts of Kindness Foundation's mission statement notes how the organization attempts to "inspire people to practice kindness and pass it on to others."[2]

At a fundamental level, acts of kindness will force you to feel better about yourself. You will put yourself in a better mood. Kindness empowers you. A positive energy is unleashed within the soul. At the very least, *being kind puts you in a positive state of mind.* Choosing to be kind will force your attitude to change. You are actually creating indispensable value for yourself. As you express kindness by choosing to share deeds of encouragement, gentleness, and politeness, the entire organization, church staff, or team will reap the rewards. When you find yourself in such an environment, you want to achieve more, you want to grow more. Thus, kindness is at the root of any individual success. Note the words of Albert Einstein:

> The ideas which have lighted my way, and time after
> time have given me new courage to face life cheerfully,
> have been kindness, beauty, and truth. The trite sub-
> jects of human efforts, possessions, outward success,
> luxury have always seemed to me contemptible.[3]

Kindness will enhance how you view yourself. So many function at mediocre levels because they fail to *see* themselves as peak performers who thrive at an optimal level. Kindness will force you to see yourself as a good person. You will begin to feel better about yourself. Your mental outlook will improve, and your performance—both personal and professional—will experience a positive flow of energy resulting in a feeling of balance, perspective, positive thoughts, and a steadfast desire to be a cheerful person of genuine goodwill to all you encounter. The power of kindness will transform your life!

Think for a moment about this question: How would being kinder transform the quality of your life? At the very least, simple acts of kindness have the potential to produce some radical results such as:

- A joyful attitude
- A positive outlook
- A peaceful mind
- A pleasant disposition

- A kind word
- A helping hand

When a person's outlook is transformed by the positive power of kindness, they begin to see themselves as useful, healthy, and valued contributors who serve humanity and work for a noble cause. Such a lofty description is a far cry from how so many workers view themselves today. The power of kindness has the potential to turn a griping, complaining, bitter, self-absorbed employee into one who develops a different mindset, thus a different lifestyle and a different way of speaking. Can you imagine a once-disgruntled employee who discovers the secrets of kind deeds?

> I really am valued, and I really do mean something to this company. My life does have worth, and my words do mean something. And although we've had cutbacks, resources are not up to date, management demands are not realistic, church members constantly criticize our decisions, and I have had to renegotiate my contract, I really do contribute something significant and meaningful and worthwhile to this organization, and I like how that makes me feel.

On a deep level, some security needs are met. Suddenly, your purpose for existence takes on added dimensions of significance. Your role is not merely to complete a task but to contribute to the overall spirit and goodwill of an organization—be it in business, on a volunteer team, at church, or at home. Teaching a university-level interpersonal communication course required an explanation of Maslow's Hierarchy of Needs.[4] Psychologist Abraham Maslow argues that human needs fall into several categories, and he notes that among a human's most basic need is safety. We need to know our well-being will be protected. Such a need is the foundation for security.

Think for a moment about how important security is. Because you feel good about who you are, you forfeit the need to be rude or ugly. You can expend your energy being kind rather than proving your worth. My father was such a kind person. Actually, I think his kindness produced a humility that personified his life. Speaker and author James Ryle makes sense of how feeling secure can produce a correlation of kindness and humility: "Humility is the God-given self-assurance that eliminates the need to prove the worth of who you are and the rightness of what you do."

Kindness ignites an energy that has the power to transform your life. In Wayne Dyer's fascinating book *Intentions*, the author quotes a study that speaks to the power of kindness. Take a moment to examine Dyer's words and reflect on the power acts of kindness can produce in your life.

The positive effect of kindness on the immune system and the increased production of serotonin in the brain has been proven in research studies. Serotonin is a naturally occurring substance in the body that makes us feel more comfortable, peaceful, and even blissful. In fact, the role of most antidepressants is to stimulate the production of serotonin chemically, helping to ease depression. Research has shown that a simple act of kindness directed toward another improves the functioning of the immune system and stimulates the production of serotonin in both the recipient of the kindness and the person extending the kindness. Even more amazing is that persons observing the act of kindness have similar beneficial results.[5]

Medical research is confirming what wise sages have known for generations: dispensing acts of kindness improves mental health. Just *observing* acts of kindness encourages a more peaceful, positive, and productive lifestyle! A third-grade dropout, who never spent a day in a psychology class, never published a paper, and never treated a patient, understood clearly how to improve one's outlook, health, and vitality. Kind deeds truly are never lost.

Think about your career for a moment. Could your professional portfolio benefit from a boost of kindness?

Think about those special relationships for a while. How would kindness enhance the quality of those relationships?

Try something. What do you have to lose? My dad often said, "Son, it does not cost a dime to be kind." Increase kindness for one week by doing the following:

1. Say "thank you" more than "I."
2. Say either "yes, please" or "no, thank you."
3. Allow others to enter buildings before you.
4. Open doors for others.
5. Talk less about yourself and listen more.
6. Allow others to board airplanes and elevators first.
7. Offer your assistance to others.
8. Offer words of encouragement to others.
9. Purposely smile at another person.
10. Help those who lack the power to reward you.

Do not be surprised if during this week of kindness you see a decrease in your rudeness, skepticism, and self-absorption. Furthermore, enjoy the week's added bonus of enhanced energy, a feeling of euphoria, greater work productivity, and a relentless sense of accomplishment and joy.

Being a kind human being transforms a self-absorbed average worker into a joyful overachiever who feels good about the effort generated to help others. Which type of boss would you prefer? Bosses, take note that if you are perceived as unkind, expect very little from employees. They will offer minimum effort and little else. Make a choice to live a lifestyle of kindness. You will transform your life and working environment with a positive energy and an infectious passion!

We have become a culture that does not say "thank you." Do not take my word for it. Go to any facility where the public is being served, and listen to how few people will offer a simple "thanks."

My favorite place to observe this trend is airport check-in counters. In fact, airports seem to be a vast wasteland when it comes to expressions of kindness. A visit with an American Airlines check-in agent revealed my unscientific observations. The agent, based in San Jose, California, said rarely is there a "thank you" from passengers. She noted how passengers are becoming more self-absorbed, mean-spirited, and eager to blame agents for delays resulting from mechanical problems and weather. The next time you are at an airport, just listen to how rude people can be! You don't even have to be at an airport! Attempt a lane change while driving in traffic!

The next time you're at a public facility, just count the times people say thanks. Count the times you observe someone helping someone else. Note the words of encouragement or helpfulness you hear. You may be shocked by how uncommon "common courtesy" has become.

Kindness is biblical, practical, and wise. You gain a reputation as being a decent human being! When you serve others with kindness, you experience the very best a day has to offer! Allowing others to proceed before you may cost you five seconds, but it adds five times the energy to your day. You do the math!

Kindness can take on many forms. For example, when communicating, your tone may speak more about you than your words. Have you ever been scolded by a superior, who used firm words but a kind tone? Conversely, have you ever been ridiculed by someone who may have used appropriate language but whose tone was demeaning and discouraging? Choosing to speak in a kind tone has the power to turn away wrath, change a mood, even transform a relationship.

Kindness may also be expressed through our listening choices. Choosing to listen actively to someone, looking them squarely in the eyes, and purposely remembering the major points may take more than the 15 seconds that defines the attention span of the average adult, but will add value and honor and dignity to the person with whom you are interacting. Contrast this with the numerous conversations we have during the day when we struggle just to remember the person's name. Helping others at airports and supermarkets may delay you for a few minutes. However, the person you help will feature you in conversation for weeks to come. Not to mention the immediate benefit you get from helping someone! Smiling at people and offering encouraging words was not something just for the television families of the 1950s. Try smiling! It takes more of an effort to sustain a frown than a smile! Right now—smile! You just begin to feel better about yourself! There's a reason children are filled with joy!

Spend this week using kind words and speaking with a kind tone. Try listening to people instead of talking over them. You will be amazed at the newfound power of your speech! Note the words of French author George Sand: "Guard well within you that treasure, kindness. Know how to give without hesitation, how to lose without regret, how to acquire without meanness."

Be kind to all people. Remember, we all are God's creation. Being kind to the least among you endears you to the heart of the Creator. Our world desperately needs people who will commit to a lifestyle of kindness. Once leaders experience the transformative power of kindness, their organizations will never be the same. Instead of a culture where leaders are in the pattern of catching people doing wrong, why not empower employees! Catching people doing things wrong is stifling and oppressive. Such managerial styles produce employees who come to work seeking just a paycheck and a parking space. Granted, there are times for evaluation. But there are also times for commendation. As leaders, make every effort to commit acts of kindness routinely. As team members, worry less about impressing others with imitations of success (words, wardrobe, and whereabouts), and focus more on impacting those around you with kindness! A simple act of kindness can turn around a career, transform a relationship, and even impact someone for a lifetime. I'll never forget one simple act committed by my father a few years back.

I was in graduate school, married with two children. Time was short and money was scarce. All of a sudden, the motor went out in our family car, and we did not have the funds to repair it. As I took the bus to school, asked for rides, or walked just about everywhere else, we pondered what to do. I finally asked my parents for help. My mother immediately bought me a one-way Amtrak train ticket from Eugene, Oregon, to Martinez, California. She told me not to worry about a thing and that I would be able to take one of their cars, drive it back to school and use it for as long as we needed it. Well just that kindness alone would have been enough. But the story does not stop there.

While at home, Dad told me that they had a late model Oldsmobile and an earlier model Cadillac. While both cars were in good running condition, the Cadillac was considerably older and not in the greatest shape. I simply assumed that I would use the Cadillac and quite frankly, was excited just to have a working vehicle. But when my father handed me the keys to the Oldsmobile, I was so stunned that I remember tearing up. I said, "Dad, I cannot take your best vehicle." He responded, "Son, I would have it no other way."

What my father chose to do may not seem all that heroic. It certainly did not make the headlines of the paper or gain mention during the local newscast. But this simple act of kindness was so powerful that it literally *has* transformed how I treat my own children. My father was not loaning me a car, he was teaching me a principle. "Son, always be as kind as you can to others—often such a sacrifice will mean giving your best away."

My father loaned us his Oldsmobile Delta '88 in 1988. We kept that car during the remainder of our graduate school days at the University of Oregon. I only had the car for two years, but the lesson will last an eternity. It is very important for me to treat my wife, my children, our family and friends with absolute kindness—and sometimes that requires a kind of sacrificial giving that is so foreign in our world today.

In retrospect, my parents were wealthy—not financially but in every other way. They were surrounded by a loving family, had

> SON, ALWAYS BE AS KIND AS YOU CAN TO OTHERS—OFTEN SUCH A SACRIFICE WILL MEAN GIVING YOUR BEST AWAY.

great friends, and lived a full life. They gave until their dying days. They gave to anyone. Anyone in need. I don't recall many Sunday dinners that featured only our family at the table. My folks always looked for someone to bless . . . someone to invest in . . . someone to be kind toward. Financial status was not an issue. Ethnicity did not matter. They were color-blind when it came to being kind. Can you think of someone like this in your life? Look at the impact they are making and the legacy they are leaving!

Dad, you will never know what a profound impact your simple act of kindness had on me. My father was a master teacher. He was the kind of teacher who was teaching even when he was not teaching.

Acts of kindness, both delivered and observed, have an amazingly powerful influence on people and within organizations. Consider the following:

THE IMPACT OF KINDNESS

1. **Kindness creates the opportunity for meaningful communication.** Now people are less concerned with "impressive" speech (speaking to sound important). They seek to connect with others for the purpose of learning and exploring. The simple task of remembering someone's name or paraphrasing a central idea indicates you have

been listening—not merely hearing (which is an automatic function)—but actively listening to the person's words. You remember major points of discussions, and you remember names. A simple interaction with another human being has now turned into a meaningful dialogue, which has potential to produce the following:

- Increase value in how others feel
- Restore dignity among workers
- Provide more authenticity in communication
- Provide significance to those involved
- Discover the purpose of talking together rather than listening just for performance

Value, dignity, authenticity, significance, purpose. Simple acts within groups generate power to impact people and cultures in dramatic fashion.

2. Kindness restores energy levels within people. Have you ever had a job where you actually *wanted* to go to work? What was so different about that job? I would argue that job duties and job problems and job issues were about the same as any found in any employment environment. The difference was—and is—the people! As sports talk show host Jim Rome once stated, "I don't want a job I have to take a two-week vacation to get away from!" There is an energy that explodes around a group of people who value each other. They are so positive that you think they could do absolutely anything! A major source of this power comes from being kind to people. When you are kind, your blood is fortified, your immune system is strengthened, you feel better physically, sharper mentally, and more agreeable socially. Being kind is analogous to eating an energy bar, going for a walk, taking a hot bath, or having a refreshing dip in cool water! Your mind and your body are infused with feelings of warmth, joy, and bliss! A peace that surpasses comprehension reigns in your soul. There is a song in your heart. You enjoy a smile on your face. There's light-heartedness despite the seriousness of the hour. Kindness produces a similar energy as a mini-vacation—without airport lines! When you're kind to people, you please God the Father, and you cannot please God without enjoying great benefit! Allow one act of kindness per day to be your *power nap* for the new millennium!

3. Kindness encourages and uplifts the spirit. Take a look around your community. You will notice people who could benefit from a little encouragement. Take teachers, for example. Elementary and high school teachers are underpaid, overworked, and under-appreciated. I see it on their faces each August when I travel the country offering motivational and convocational speeches for faculty celebrating the new academic year. If teachers need anything, they need encouragement—they need their spirits uplifted.

As I travel from church to church sharing God's word, I enjoy the opportunity to fellowship with pastors and their spouses. Typically, a pastor is heavily burdened, overworked, stressed to the max, and near burnout. It should come as no surprise.

As I journey from company to company—whether the local utility company or the *Fortune* 500 corporation—I observe similar trends. Executives scratching their heads for answers, middle managers exhausted from being stretched in many ways, and employee groups working for pay rather than pride, performance, and pleasure. These companies do not need more technology. Organizations are in critical need of an infusion of kindness to strengthen the immune system and boost energy levels! Just a little kindness executed each day will boost the morale of an environment in ways a new computer never could!

Kindness is personally and professionally transforming. A simple act of kindness can change your mood, alter your day, even affect how you rear your children. The April 11, 2005 issue of *Time* magazine is a commemorative publication to the life and legacy of Pope John Paul II. What struck me was how the simple respect and kindness of one man impacted millions. Monsignor

Lorenzo Albacete, a friend of the Pope, summed up his life beautifully:

> John Paul II knows that no one reads the encyclicals of a dead pope. That is why he has taken to the streets. It can only last a minute, but you'd think people had 10 hours of the most intimate mystical experience. For many people, it is that one moment when they say, "I saw another possibility in life."[6]

A most critical question to ask is this: What do people feel like after they have been in your presence? Do they walk away saying, "I saw another possibility in life?" Or do they depart undaunted, unaffected, and none the better?

Today is a marvelous opportunity to begin speaking kindly to people. This is your opportunity to share a kind act with another person. That third-grade dropout is correct when he says, "Kind deeds are never lost!" Try a little kindness. Your small effort will go a long way!

CHAPTER 3

AN HOUR EARLY

LESSONS ON DISCIPLINE

There is a move in society that is causing some to scratch their heads. More and more companies are abandoning conventional wisdom and instead are re-thinking hiring decisions. These companies are not recruiting the gifted college graduate. Rather, they are selecting retirees with no age limit! During a *60 Minutes* broadcast, company managers justified their reasons for encouraging the sixty-plus population to return to the workforce. Several gerontology studies—the scientific study of the process of aging—confirm that Americans are living longer and want alternatives from traditional modes of retirement. And while there are those who enjoy the relaxed pace of retirement, a segment of older Americans found themselves disillusioned with "doing nothing."

What companies who employ older workers discover is both predictable and profound. The workers are dependable, honest, possess a strong work ethic, and are on time! While the report noted a few challenges associated with hiring older Americans, the advantages they bring to the job far exceed any concerns employees may have voiced.

These workers represent a population of people who lived off the land. They survived the Great Depression, defended our borders during world wars, and rebuilt the country's infrastructure in post-war America. This population of American citizens planted the seeds that produced the greatest technological revolution in the history of humankind and produced the greatest superpower in the world. And, they did it with promptness, honesty, integrity, diligence, and hard work!

You may know people like this. What are your impressions of them? Do you find them loyal, dependable, and hardworking? How have they impacted your life? How have they influenced your work environment? What difference have they made in your family life?

Conversely, have you ever been associated with someone who was always late? No matter what the circumstance or situation, you knew they were going to be late! They are never on time. Never. You accept it for the first few times, but now you're asking yourself, "Why do I tolerate this behavior?" How do you feel about people like this? Bestselling author John Mason once observed, "One sure way to make a negative lasting impression is to waste someone's time!"

I wish I had a dime for every time my father said,

"Son, you would rather be an hour early than a minute late." Believe me, this was not just a phrase. Dad meant it, and he practiced it. My father was a cook at California Maritime Academy (CMA) in Vallejo, California, located just thirty miles north of San Francisco and about fifteen minutes from our home. Today, CMA continues to educate and train midshipmen for careers in the maritime industry. From the 1950s through his retirement decades later, my Dad worked the breakfast and lunch shift beginning at five o'clock in the morning until one o'clock in the afternoon.

According to Mother, Dad was never late in his three decades at CMA. He believed that a person ought to keep his or her word, and if you promise to be someplace at a certain time, then you are there. No excuses. No justifications relating to traffic, road construction, oversleeping, or other "personal issues" which may have resulted in tardiness. While military training no doubt influenced his choices, my Dad had an inner clock. He believed in arriving early. His belief in arriving early was so strong that to assure the promptness of my mother (to Mother, time was a magazine!) *every* clock in our home was set at least ten minutes ahead of the actual time!

Arriving early speaks to a value reflective of an era gone by. Just a generation ago, when people were not so self-absorbed, workers and worshipers were on time! If you began work at five o'clock in the morning, then you were likely there at least a half-hour early.

What was my dad communicating to his family? What lesson was he trying to teach my brother and me? Upon years of thinking about his phrase on time, struggling with my own promptness, and returning to his words, I see clearly what Dad's central message was. My dad's wisdom lesson had less to do with time, and more to do with discipline and self-control. Using his lesson as a starting point will allow for the unpacking of a life-changing concept.

We live in a culture where discipline has eroded far from the consciousness of everyday thought. Yesterday, the old folks would speak of possessing common sense. Such sense—which is no longer common—is rooted in the disciplined life of generations of Americans who had little or no choice but to be their best.

Think about this for a moment. The beauty of my father's ideas is they were not limited to the idea itself! My father was a master teacher in that he used one concept to teach several. My father was not merely teaching timeliness, but the basic art and science of discipline.

Discipline is defined in Webster's Dictionary as "a training that develops self-control, character, or orderliness and efficiency; a self-controlled or orderly conduct." Self-control, character, orderliness, and efficiency. I have just described the elders in the neighborhood where I grew up. I have just described the little league coaches and the den mothers, the schoolteachers and the youth leaders. I just described Mrs. Candice Vigen, my junior high school journalism teacher. I just described Coach Wes Matthews, the best baseball coach I ever had (and the vice principal for Springstown Junior High School in Vallejo, California). I just described Mr. Shirley H. Day, my high school Sunday school teacher at Good Samaritan Missionary Baptist Church, Vallejo, California. Brother Day—a teacher among teachers—was the only person who made me *want* to go to Sunday school! I just described Philmore Graham, director of the Continentals of Omega Boys Club, Vallejo, California. He is the type of man whose impact lasts for a lifetime. I have just described Roxie Johnson and Audrey and Fay Thompson, Sr., next-door neighbors who were like second parents. Back then, parents and neighbors were not running popularity contests. They were about the business of rearing children and turning them into responsible adults.

You want to talk about discipline! I'll give you another definition. When I was growing up, all of the above-mentioned individuals had personal invitations from my parents to reinforce "proper behavior" if needed. I must comment to my younger readers that I envy your methods of discipline today. Trust me, we did not have "time-outs" in the 1950s and 1960s, although I could time how long

I was knocked out! My parents—as was the case with many on the 1100 block of Louisiana Street in Vallejo, California—would send you to a tree to select a "switch" for your own spanking! These were the longest walks of my life! I never wanted to return home! Just like Forrest Gump, I wanted to keep walking—to the next state!

A familiar African proverb states, "It takes an entire village to raise one child." My community—black, white, Jewish, Hispanic, Polish, Russian, and Asian—lived this proverb. Not everyone graduated from the community discipline academy with flying colors. This is not the point. Clearly, just four decades ago, there was a climate in society—a culture—that encouraged self-control, character, orderliness and efficiency.

IN THIS POST-MODERN ERA, STYLE POINTS ARE VALUED AND CHARACTER POINTS ARE VILIFIED.

And many of the elders not only aspired to reflect those attributes, they believed it was their duty and obligation to pass on those traits to a waiting generation of baby boomers. One such elder was Roger Marion Rigsby.

The essence of my father was discipline. I recall the little things in his life that reflected self-control and order. There was a certain way he would tie his shoes. There was a certain way he would care for his guns. There was a certain way he would care for his cars. I hear his voice ringing in my mind with a piercing familiarity:

> Son, make sure that oil is changed every 3,000 miles. Rotate those tires every 6,000 miles. Check your tires before every entry into your car. Never drive a car beyond a quarter tank of gas—not good for the engine. Always keep your tools clean, and keep these in your trunk: a flashlight, some rope, and a blanket.

Isn't it strange how yesterday's boring, redundant, and routine lectures from parents produce tears in your eyes today? Dad was teaching about more than being on time. His generation was passing the torch to a new generation. And the lessons are inescapable. To this very day—much to my family's amusement—I still kick the tires before each trip. I still check the back seat before unlocking the car door. I never allow my gas tank to register below the one-quarter mark.

Self-control, character, orderliness, and efficiency. How would your career change if you developed these traits with the same passion and exuberance as you develop style and image? In this post-modern era, style points are valued and character points are vilified.

Such a societal landscape encourages the instant gratification of her citizens. It may take Coach Matthews forty years to impact a mediocre baseball catcher named Ricky Rigsby. Nobody has that kind of time, especially when you can wear a nice suit of clothing and immediately make an impression.

Dad had the time. He made time. And, to this day I am so grateful. I am grateful for the lessons he tried to instill. My father never officially proclaimed that school was in session and lessons were to be learned. We caught the lessons—largely by his example in front of us.

I think about how he tried to teach efficiency and order, for example, by the way he would prepare food in his spare time. Occasionally, Dad would cater wedding receptions and other events for those in our church who could not afford the more expensive caterers. With no commercial kitchen, no large staff, and very few culinary conveniences, my father created masterpieces! His cooking was the talk of the town! While all enjoyed the food, few saw the order and efficiency that produced the excellence.

If the event was Saturday afternoon, my father began his cooking preparation immediately following work Friday afternoon. Everything from shrimp to sauces, cheeses, and greens had their place. There was a schedule for each preparation. There was a protocol for every kitchen maneuver. Saying very little, but working with his customary focus and intent, I noticed how effortlessly things came together—a sure sign of professionalism at the highest level. He made cooking for large groups look so easy. During chats in between preps, Dad might say, "Son, this crab salad has to have the perfect mixture of mayonnaise, celery, and salt. The salad cannot just look good, it must taste good." *Dad, you were teaching—even when I had no clue. I'll never be able to thank you.*

Think for a moment about all the simple yet profound lessons you "caught" from your parents. Re-member, the ideas your parents attempted to share were not limited to the ideas themselves. Your parents were using the experiences and adventures from their world to communicate to you timeless values they hoped and prayed would someday help you to impact this world!

DISCIPLINE INFLUENCES ENDURANCE

Do you remember when you were a child and your mother would tell you, "Just grin and bear it"? Mother was communicating that a disciplined lifestyle will carry you through even the most difficult of circumstances. Discipline is a wonderful elixir for a culture desperately seeking depth and purpose amidst the enfranchisement of superficiality. In other words, ours is an age that would rather *feel* disciplined than actually *be* disciplined.

Roderick Hart, a distinguished scholar at the University of Texas, noted that in American culture you do not have to know about politics. Rather, simply *feeling* as though you know about world affairs will appease your sense of civic responsibility.[7] Hart's assessment is not only accurate but may be applied to other venues within our society's landscape. In our culture, just offering the image of knowledge has replaced building a knowledge base. A culture which lacks discipline sees no need to know how to accomplish or resolve or complete. If one can merely *feel* as though they can accomplish something, it eliminates the desire to actually hang in there and battle through the tough places necessary for success.

> YOUR PARENTS WERE USING THE EXPERIENCES AND ADVENTURES FROM THEIR WORLD TO COMMUNICATE TO YOU TIMELESS VALUES THEY HOPED AND PRAYED WOULD SOMEDAY HELP YOU TO IMPACT THIS WORLD!

Discipline forces you to grin and bear it. You cannot go or leave or come back or try later. You have to stay—to remain—to wait. You're forced to figure, to contemplate, to meditate, to rearrange, to refigure. To think. How many times have you begged for extra time to just think more.

The great misconception in modern society is that finishing first is best. As a college professor, I see this pattern among many students who would rather send "the signal of success" by being among the first to complete an exam rather than toiling over the accuracy of the work. Such a delusional view of success is robbing young and old of the stuff required for success—time, struggle, evaluation, reevaluation, even failure.

To suggest that one can accomplish any measure of success without discipline is to suggest that a plane can fly without engines. Discipline powers your life with the additive of endurance—a quality of life that will cause you to earn more money, get more jobs, sell more accounts, and realize more dreams simply because you didn't quit. Winston Churchill said it best when addressing a graduating college class in the United States. I first saw his entire six-word speech as a young reporter assigned to cover the San Francisco Giants baseball team in the late 1970s. On the wall of the tunnel that connected the Giants' locker room to the dugout at Candlestick Park were the simple words: "Never, Never, Never, Never Give Up." Six words that live in infamy in terms of global impact, and arguably resulted in the most memorable commencement speech in the history of the spoken word! Six words that are not taught as high school or college curriculum. Six words that rarely are bantered about the water cooler. Six words that are not daily reminders, nor part of pop culture, nor mentioned by most. Six words that have the potential to transform a corporate culture, a company's morale, and a family's mood.

The explosive power of discipline will produce in humans an insatiable desire to stretch farther, climb higher, study smarter, run faster, grow smarter. My father showed me that a disciplined life creates greater freedom in life. Your life has order and purpose. Your efficiency level increases as your productivity soars to greater heights. You begin noticing that arriving early is changing how you view the world. Slowly at first, then gaining in momentum, you realize you are attending to tasks and chores with greater efficiency. You embrace the concept of excellence as a lifestyle. Impacting your world is no longer a concept, but a way of life!

Roger Rigsby's morning shift at CMA began at five o'clock in the morning. The CMA campus was approximately a fifteen-minute drive from our home in Central Vallejo, California. Dad would leave home at 3:45 A.M., arriving at CMA one full hour ahead of his shift. For years I thought the value of Dad's behavior was the obvious. But the real genius of my father's discipline was what was produced as a result. The quality of endurance was a hallmark in Dad's life. He never quit. It was Dad's lifestyle. I invite you to visit with men and women of this era (my father would have been 86 the year this book is published). Revealed on their faces and replicated in their stories is this value of endurance. Quitting does not win wars. Quitting does not feed families. Quitting does not build champions or produce winners. Quitting does not rebuild New York following 9/11. Quitting does not take the ice against the Soviet Union in 1980. Quitting does not ride with Lance Armstrong through the rugged terrain of France. Quitting does not advance your career, improve your performance, bless your spouse, or impress your children. Quitting creates constant upheaval and destructive turmoil. Quitting rips apart the fabric of a family. Quitting shuns responsibility and ignores commitments. Quitting almost always results in chaos, devastation, decline, and failure. Are you ready to commit in your mind and resolve in your heart to live a life of discipline? Your commitment will return on your investment the added bonus of endurance. Almost immediately you will discover its power and added benefit in your life!

A life of discipline has the power to transform a person from an impressionable existence to one who makes an impact. Revealed in the dimensions of disciplined living is the quality of honor and the potential to live an honorable life. During the four decades I knew my father, I observed a behavior that captured a dynamic marriage between endurance and honor.

When you talk to people born during the first four decades of the twentieth century, you discover an unusual quality rarely displayed among citizens of the new millennium. Imbedded in their consciousness is this belief that you just don't quit. Indelibly etched on the hearts of such folks is the notion that if you tell someone you're going to do something, you do it—no matter what the cost, no matter how early, no matter what the hardship is for you. Honor is born in the heart when your words are consistent with your actions. Establishing core values, speaking those values, and living by those

HONOR IS BORN IN THE HEART WHEN YOUR WORDS ARE CONSISTENT WITH YOUR ACTIONS.

values produces a consistency that reveals a quality of life rarely on display in present culture. My father's generation simply and unwittingly said what they meant and meant what they said. Listen to the language of their generation:

- Talk is cheap.
- Actions speak louder than words.
- Your word is your bond.
- Don't say it if you don't mean it.

Contrast these words with the language that consumes our culture today:

- Learn to talk a good game.
- All things are negotiable and subject to change.

- Never promise what you cannot deliver.
- Well, I showed up didn't I?
- Just do the best you can.
- Oh well, you tried didn't you?

Inherent in the earlier generation of people was the belief that an honorable life was contingent upon an unfailing commitment to personal discipline. However, our generation has misplaced our allegiance to discipline and instead embraced convenience.

Try being a person of character without personal discipline. Try accomplishing anything of great value without personal discipline. Discipline is the engine that powers your entire life. Moreover, discipline provides the necessary parameters for order, structure, purpose, and freedom—all of which are dimensions of character.

Discipline means subjecting yourself to rigorous and intense scrutiny, evaluation, and practice that inevitably will result in your life being enhanced. Simply choosing to live a disciplined lifestyle sets you apart from those who see no need to subject themselves to anything whether it's for their good or not.

One may do well to revisit an era when life was not lived for show. You did your best because that was the expectation. You did what you said because that was the expectation. You took pride in doing a good job and gained the respect of peers for fulfilling your obligations and responsibilities. In the process you learned what it meant to be an honorable person—one whose life displayed an indefatigable consistency between values, words, and actions.

An attempt to sustain excellence without self-discipline tragically undermines personal growth. Arguably, discipline is chief among the attributes of success. Show me someone who achieves at a high level—regardless of profession or task—and I will show you someone committed to the pursuit of self-discipline. Speaking of such a commitment among early Christian workers, nineteenth-century missionary Martyn Lloyd-Jones observed:

> I defy you to read the life of any saint that has ever adorned the life of the Church without seeing at once that the greatest characteristic in the life of that saint was discipline and order. Invariably it is the universal characteristic of all the outstanding men and women of God. . . . Obviously it is something that is thoroughly scriptural and absolutely essential.[8]

Roger Marion Rigsby was early to all events and engagements. The early arrival was the outward expression of an unwavering commitment to promote a lifestyle that made self-discipline among his most cherished and valued possessions.

What would your life look like if you made a choice every day to be an hour early? While it may be impractical to follow such a mandate to the letter, how about embracing the spirit of the lesson? How might your professional life improve if you were early to every appointment from this point on? Would you be more influential as a leader, a mentor, a husband, or a student?

One of my best friends is Rev. Paul Holderfield, Jr., senior pastor of Friendly Chapel Church of the Nazarene in North Little Rock, Arkansas. Each summer for the past several years, I have been privileged to speak during the church's annual revival services. Brother Paul—as he is affectionately known—has put up with my antics, and my tardiness. Typically, if a service began at 6:00 P.M., I would arrive at . . . 6:00 P.M.—maybe even a few minutes after. Brother Paul never said a word, but I knew it bothered him.

Recently I felt convicted to start applying Dad's lesson on arriving early in every possible situation. It has transformed my professional life and, more importantly, influenced personal relationships. When I announced to Brother Paul that I would be arriving to each service an hour prior to the beginning of service, he began to weep and commented, "Rick, that's the best gift you could have ever given me."

Is there a *gift* you need to give someone at work, at home, or at church? Are you feeling convicted right now about the habit of lateness you allowed to creep into your personal and professional life? Do you find that discipline is declining in other areas of your life as well? Perhaps it's time to give the *gift* that a disciplined life produces. You cannot imagine the impact something as simple as showing up early can have on another person.

Thank you, Dad, for teaching me the simple lesson of arriving an hour early. I finally got it. I saw how arriving early impacted another person. Brother Paul sends his thanks as well!

CHAPTER 4

HELPING OTHERS

LESSONS ON BUILDING COMMUNITY

Imagine for a moment growing up in the 1960s. Life was rather simple. If your parents told you to jump, you said, "How high?" This is not to suggest that we did not have our rebellious moments! However, make no mistake about it, in the Rigsby home, the parents were the law, and most days, the law won!

Among our favorite shows during this era of television was *Batman*. This mid-sixties classic featured an array of stars from Adam West and Bert Ward to Caesar Romero, Burgess Meredith, and Eartha Kitt as Catwoman. *Batman* was technologically revolutionary for two reasons in our home. First, the program was "in color" which meant big-time entertainment. Second, the show aired on two consecutive nights—part one Wednesday, and part two Thursday. *Wow! Bam! Wham!*

Even the power of *Batman* could not keep my parents from volunteering us to help someone. Dad did not care what was on television; if it was time to help, we helped! And, for some strange reason, it seemed as though the times our parents really wanted our help were Wednesdays and Thursdays around seven in the evening! Many nights the Caped Crusaders were forced to battle evil without me because my parents were issuing a higher calling.

Go back for a moment to the mid-sixties. It's Wednesday at 7:00 P.M. And even though our small house does not offer many luxuries, we do have a home theater system! Let me explain.

If you were born before 1960, it's likely that your parents had one of those long—and I do mean *long*—RCA stereos. There was a record player right in the middle. For those of you born after 1970, a record is a vinyl disc with one continual groove! Next to the record player was a television set complete with a picture tube. How many of you remember that it would take thirty seconds for the set to warm up and display a picture? And what a beautiful picture it was! It was the mid-sixties. We were watching *Star Trek*, *Gilligan's Island*, *Get Smart*, and *Batman* . . . in color!

Right as *Batman* was beginning, I can still hear my mother calling, "Ricky, go down the street and help Mr. Wilson move some wood. He's not feeling well and could really use your help. It will only take about an hour, then you can come home, take a bath, and get ready for bed."

"Mother, may I watch *Batman*, then go help?"

"Boy, take your fat butt down the street and do what I told you to do!"

I may have lived in the San Francisco Bay Area, but I had *southern* parents. And when they said, "Jump," we asked, "How high?" In my day, you did not "negotiate" with your parents. There was no back talk, no "time-outs," no sympathy. In my house, you knew that any wrong move on your part would result in some intimate fellowship with a belt strap!

When my parents said "help," their voices were legitimate because they practiced what they preached. My parents, like other parents of this era, represented a generation of helpers—what I refer to as a generation of doers. We have become a generation of *viewers*. We talk a good game when it comes to helping, but there's no follow-through if we sense the slightest degree of inconvenience.

Think for a moment about the parents of the previous generation. Most worked dawn to dusk. Many worked two jobs, yet you heard little complaining. But if a friend was in need, help was on the way! This generation was comprised of folks

> MY PARENTS, LIKE OTHER PARENTS OF THIS ERA, REPRESENTED A GENERATION OF HELPERS—WHAT I REFER TO AS A GENERATION OF DOERS.

who were reliable, dependable, and willing to serve. We have slid backwards a bit over the last half century.

How would your influence as a leader grow if you increased helping others just ten percent of the time? How would your reputation be enhanced if you were known as the employee who helped others before helping yourself? How would your status among family and friends improve if they discovered you helping rather than caught you acting selfishly?

Helping someone else is so powerful that it can change a life forever. Just ask Rev. Billy Graham to tell you about his life-long helper—the late T.W. Wilson.

Friends since childhood, Graham and Wilson answered a call to serve the Lord throughout the world. Early on, it became apparent that Rev. Graham would need the ultimate helper—one who was selfless, uninterested in personal attention, not a showboat or seeker of fame, and above all someone so sold on Christ that no task would be beneath him.

On page 19 of Jay Dennis' outstanding book *Leading with Billy Graham: The Leadership Principles and Life of T. W. Wilson*, Dennis writes:

> For almost forty years T. W. Wilson was Mr. Graham's best friend, traveling companion, bodyguard, and executive assistant, handling every detail of his demanding

schedule. Their friendship began when they were teen-agers growing up in Charlotte, North Carolina. You will be fascinated and encouraged by T. W.'s next-level influence whether dealing with presidents or prisoners; celebrities or caretakers; princes or preachers.[9]

Dennis interviews numerous people who help validate Wilson's helping spirit. One such person was Don Bailey, a Billy Graham associate and one of Wilson's many friends. Bailey added, "Billy trusts T.W. implicitly. He could say exactly what he thought to Billy. T knew about his sched-ule, where he needed to be, the mundane, his luggage—all of these things, T did in such a Christlike spirit. He put aside his own needs to meet Billy's needs" (p. 171).

But the most powerful words come from Evelyn Freeland, Wilson's long-time assistant who said, "He was a number one man content with a number two position." Dennis concludes by adding, "T. W. realized that there was no higher calling than that of a servant" (p. 176).

What kind of influence would your life reflect if today you began realizing that there was no higher calling than that of a servant? The power at your disposal would be supernatural. Your presence would be so powerful that you would not only influence people within your circles, but you would impact generations for eternity. All because you made a choice to develop a servant's mentality.

If our work environments are going to change for the positive, then we need to see leaders with a servant's heart. If our families have any chance at all, then family members must reconnect to a servant's heart. If our culture has any hope of moving from the superficial malaise of self-absorption, then we must be willing to embrace the simple life of a servant.

THE HIGH CALL OF HELPING

There is something divine about helping others. The very essence of helping is rooted in the heart of God. As you help people, you move away from the shackles of independence and self-absorption. Granted, there are times to be independent. But with all the needs in the world, who wants to be so independent that you contribute nothing to the lives of others?

Think about some of the world's greatest helpers: Mother Teresa, Mahatma Gandhi, the Good Samaritan. What is it about their lives that mark them as uniquely significant? Each possesses that one rare quality among humans—the desire to move beyond the self.

Now, think for a moment about the people who have influenced you. Not the scores of friends you have, but the one or two who really impacted your life. At their core, they were helpers. Servants. People who gave, shared, encouraged, and helped in any way possible.

I recall the first Christmas after my precious wife died from breast cancer. My two sons and I were not doing so well. For the first time in forever, cards were not mailed, stockings were not hung, and a tree was not trimmed. I shall never forget when some friends came by to help. What was remarkable was they did not ask to help nor did they make an appointment. They stopped by one evening, made some popcorn, put on some Christmas carols, pulled all the decorations out of the closets, and in just a few hours transformed our holiday gloom with some warm moments and fond memories.

IF OUR CULTURE HAS ANY HOPE OF MOVING FROM THE SUPERFICIAL MALAISE OF SELF-ABSORPTION, THEN WE MUST BE WILLING TO EMBRACE THE SIMPLE LIFE OF A SERVANT.

What is of importance here is the principle applied. If you *ask* to help, chances are you are the only one who will be blessed! People tend to express their gratitude, and politely decline your offer. But you'll feel good for asking! However, when you see a need and fulfill it, then the individual is surprised, thrilled, awed, and blessed beyond measure. As for you, your blessing just intensified! You feel good about yourself and look forward to the opportunity to help someone else.

Often we are willing to help but our motivation is wrong. If you volunteer to help for any reason other than to bless the recipient, then an element of deception has polluted your intention.

The best helpers—the very best helpers—are silent, quiet, and unassuming. They work for the sole purpose of coming to the aid of another. They do not wait around to hear "thank you" or seek adulation and applause, nor do they require a showcase to display their work. An authentic helper moves beyond the realm of self-absorption. The mission of such a worker is to help; the goal is not to impress, but to impact!

Think about it for a moment. Have you ever been surprised by someone at a restaurant who paid your tab without you knowing? The surprise and joy felt is simply exhilarating. Conversely, has someone ever "announced" to the entire restaurant that they are paying your bill? Joy and exhilaration do not immediately come to mind!

Those born in the early part of the twentieth century represent a generation of helpers. During war and peace, feast and famine, necessity mandated your help. Society expected you to help. When I was a child, the last person my parents called was the repairman. If Mom or Dad could not fix something, a relative or friend came to the rescue. People looked out for each other, seemed more concerned about the welfare of others, and did whatever they could to assist people. We behaved differently a half-century ago. Helping was what it meant to be part of a family, a neighborhood, and a community. We grew up with the expectation that helping your fellow human being was a privilege. From television commercials promising, "you can trust your car to the man who wears the star," to federally funded programs such as the Peace Corps, we were served a menu of constant reminders that citizens were *expected* to help other people. Saturday was not a day off. Sunday was not a day just for church and retreat. Those were days that you helped family and friends. Amazingly, helping often resulted in festive occasions. After you painted, food appeared and laughter ignited. After you helped friends move in, people gathered for fellowship and fun. We did not realize it at the time, but we were building value. We were building honor. We were building community. All through the act of helping. It's been said that you can't help others without helping yourself. If you help someone to the top of the mountain, then you'll find yourself at the top also!

IRONICALLY, EVEN THOUGH TODAY WE ALL HAVE MORE, WE SEEM TO HELP LESS.

We baby boomers grew up watching parents scrape, struggle, and help. Ironically, even though today we all have more, we seem to help less. With all our material success, isn't it interesting how our parents were richer? Mom and Dad, as well as those in our neighborhood, always had a sense of joy and accomplishment from helping. The effort put them in better moods. Whether it was through the church, work, little league, Cub Scouts, or high school band, if you lived in my home, you were going to help people. Whether picking sweet potatoes, washing cars, or cleaning toilets, you were going to help! Little did I realize at the time that our parents were instilling important principles through their work.

PRACTICAL PRINCIPLES FROM A LIFE OF HELPING

I can hear my dad's voice ringing in my mind with a piercing familiarity, "Son, always put yourself in a position to help somebody else." My father was a master teacher when it came to sharing life's important lessons. A master teacher does not merely talk. A master teacher offers a lesson, models the lesson, then leads the student experientially through the lesson. An article appearing in *Harvard Business Review* noted that "lecture" is the most ineffective type of teaching, while observing and guiding one's experiences through learning models produces deeper levels of learning and retention.[10] With no college degree, the third-grade dropout got it! He understood how to impact

and influence his children. From his model and our partic-
ipation as helpers, we learned these timeless lessons:

1. Helping people forces you to move beyond yourself.
You may find it difficult to be self-absorbed when you're
in the process of helping others! As you take small steps
to help a coworker, you are making giant strides, moving
away from self and toward being an authentic person. If
our world is looking for anything today, we are looking
for human beings who reflect a genuine authenticity.

2. Helping people restores value in a culture. One of
the reasons we are such an impressionistic society today
is that we have lost the joy and value of helping others.
The value of helping others is manifested in both a corporate and individual sense. First, helping others meets
a pragmatic need. Simultaneously, helping restores family, community, team, and partnership. Helping reminds
us that we need each other—that everyone has a role to
play—that everyone can contribute to something greater
than themselves and take pride in their effort. When you
are fatigued at the end of the day due to emptying yourself from investing in another, the feeling is euphoric! Any
effort that moves you beyond the crippling paradigm of
self-absorption will encourage you to make an impact
instead of just an impression!

3. Helping others releases a positive energy! What
occurs in the minds of people when they see you helping?

When a leader is perceived as a helper, the entire culture benefits. The notion that the leader would not ask you to do anything he or she would not do is powerful energy. Also, when you see your leader possessing an attitude that all labor has value, that no task is too small or beneath them, the desire to replicate that behavior is fostered in your heart. Helping releases a positive energy that creates feelings of goodwill and camaraderie, while breaking down barriers of distance, alienation, and exclusivity.

When you examine our society, it is easy to speculate why we have departed from a community of helpers. We live in a culture that would prefer to make an impression rather than an impact. Rarely would one find the words *helper* and *impression* in the same sentence. The goal of our present culture is to appear as though we are a helper. After all, who has the time or the resources? Besides, you cannot trust people anymore! And so, helping has been banished from our lifestyle and our language, while we strive to look good, sound smart, and appear appealing. After all, the goal is for people to like us!

Conversely, when you commit to a lifestyle of helping people, the focus is on them! Often, efforts will go unnoticed and unreported. Helping does not occur on a stage. Helping occurs in the garage, in the backyard, out of view of spectators, in closets, under sinks, at the computer, under the car hood, in the church kitchen, and so forth. There are no executive retreats featuring bonuses and offering incentives for employees who excel in helping. Few classes focus on how citizens may help others. The yellow pages do not advertise for people willing to help for free. In fact, if someone approached you and said they were volunteering their day to help, your second response would be suspicion (your first response would be fainting!). The community of helping is a long distance from the blare of the crowd and the glare of the lights! And so, helping—regardless of its nobility—is a tough sell in a post-modern world where people have become accustomed to and profit from talking about, marketing, promoting, and showcasing themselves.

This was not Roger Rigsby. A helper was the essence of who my father was. I can recall day after day, night after night that my father would help people. His help was not predicated upon how much you paid him or how available he was. "Son, always put yourself in a position to help somebody. Your job is to look for people to help. You'll find great joy in helping others to their feet."

Dad led by example. He was not much on words. He used his head and his hands, but his heart led him. And what a servant's heart he had.

Whether it was assisting with coaches, doing laundry around the house, helping a friend with a painting job, or working in someone else's home, we watched parents help others. When we were old enough, we participated and gained valuable experiences.

I learned from a third-grade dropout that helping has immense value. Helping is honorable. Helping restores dignity. Helping builds community. The very nature of helping calls into question the issue of self-absorption. As a result, helping others may be the most important element of team building that a coach, educator, executive, or clergy leader can foster. At the root of team is the removal of "I." If the leader of a team—whether a sales force or church staff—can influence team members to move beyond "I" and function in a manner that promotes the concept of team, opinions are respected, contributions are valued, members are valued, and what once was a loose group of individuals becomes a true team. The genesis of a development is encouraging individuals to help each other.

At the start of the 2004 collegiate football season, the Texas A&M head football coach, Dennis Franchione, decided the game jerseys worn by players would no longer include their last names on the back. He wanted his players to come together as a team and play for the name on the *front* of the jersey. Coach Fran's decision delivered a strong statement to our athletes, "We are not a group of individuals who play for the purpose of seeking our own glory. We are a team who plays for each other and our university." I am convinced that Coach Fran's action will impact those players for the rest of their lives. There really is no such thing as a self-made man.

Each person on this earth is part of a team. A basic fundamental truth is that we need each other. Those football players were reminded during a brief moment in their young lives that any success they have in life will likely be the result of and stem from everybody helping one another.

Take a brief look at all your success. Next, count all the people who helped you achieve your success. Where would you be if it were not for people who took time and exerted energy to offer help? Do you want to enjoy more success in your life? Sow the seeds of helping others! You will discover greater purpose and a richer and more rewarding life. You will feel better about yourself, which will encourage you to do more to help others. Most of all, you are recreating that strong sense of community—people helping people—that makes a neighborhood, football team, church, or corporation strong and vibrant and valued!

My dad was a very wise man. "Son, always put yourself in a position to help somebody else." Interestingly, it has taken me over four decades and three college degrees to understand what Dad was saying. If I have listened clearly and accurately, this is what he meant:

Son, you have a marvelous opportunity to build value
in those around you by looking for ways to help

humanity. Remember, no job is beneath you, no task is too unimportant to be left incomplete. Look for those you can help, and your life will be rich with exhilarating experiences, fond memories, and boundless energy from the satisfaction of assisting others. Most of all, the people you help will be grateful, honored, and blessed. My son, there is no higher calling than to reach down and pull another up. Helping is biblical, practical, and in great demand today. Always make time to help another person!

My dad may not have possessed academic intelligence. I would argue he had something greater. His experiences taught him wisdom. His life revealed clearly that one of the greatest sources of joy for him was to lend a hand to another.

It's a simple lesson from a third-grade dropout. And, if applied on a continual basis, you may find yourself impacting your home, your church, your place of employment, your community, and your world!

CHAPTER 5

IF YOU'RE GOING TO DO A JOB . . .

LESSONS ON EXCELLENCE

The hallmark of my father's life was his incessant proclivity for excellence and his undeniable intolerance for mediocrity. To this day, I hear his voice with a piercing familiarity: "Son, if you're going to do a job, do it right!" Nothing further needed to be mentioned. Dad did not believe in slothful, lazy, mediocre, average, or adequate performance. If you do something—he would say—you must take pride in it. And how can a man take pride in something that is not his absolute very best? There was no compromise here. There was no shortcut here. There was no gold medal for *just getting by* or special ribbon for *finishing first*. At the very least, a good job was expected. And if we did not do our best, we repeated the task until it met my father's standard of excellence.

One of my favorite stories about excellence comes from a speech delivered by Dr. Martin Luther King, Jr. in March 1968. Just a month later, Dr. King would be assassinated while standing on the balcony of the Lorraine Hotel in Memphis, Tennessee.

King was originally called to Memphis to encourage striking sanitation workers, who felt they were being treated unfairly by city officials. King challenged the garbage collectors to strive for the highest standard of excellence—regardless of their working conditions. In part, this is what he told those city employees:

> All labor has value. If you're a street sweeper, sweep streets the way Michelangelo painted pictures. Sweep streets the way Beethoven composed music. Sweep streets the way Shakespeare wrote poetry. Sweep streets in such a profound way that the Host of Heaven will say, "There goes a great street sweeper!"

It's interesting to note what King *did not* tell his audience that day. For example, Michelangelo, who lay suspended underneath the ceiling of the Sistine Chapel at the Vatican in Rome painting a masterpiece, was legally blind! Furthermore, it's of interest that Beethoven was legally deaf!

There's an interesting principle emerging here. Often, true greatness is revealed in weakness. Despite problems, regardless of challenges, and in the midst of extreme circumstances, Michelangelo and Beethoven both impacted the world and continue to influence generations. They never saw their "handicaps" as an excuse for mediocrity.

Pastor Jentzen Franklin put it best when he said that if you can find the faith to move beyond and get over your perceived shortcomings, even your worst liability has the potential to become your greatest asset!

Roger Rigsby taught the very same principle. Everything Dad did focused on excellence and not conditions. We did not have the latest painting equipment, but when we were charged with a painting job, that job was performed with meticulous care. We did not have a John Deere tractor or a Briggs & Stratton riding lawnmower. But when it was time to do yard work, there was a standard—and we knew what my father's standard was.

Where are the fathers and mothers today who are teaching excellence? Have we become so busy in our pursuit of things that we are guilty of ignoring the main things? Hal Himmelstein says the television is turned on in the average American home seven hours per day![11] Eric Schlessor notes that by the time a child reaches the age of eighteen, that child has watched an average of 25,000 hours of television shows and 30,000 television commercials![12] Is it possible that we have turned over the teaching duties for our children to television stars, movie producers, and video game designers? Is this where our children are learning excellence?

The time is now to stop blaming television shows and video games. The time is now to summon up the courage to take the time and the interest to not only talk about excellence, but display excellence. If ever our children needed an alternative education, now is that time!

I recall a speaking engagement in Stockton, California, for "at-risk" high school students who were quickly running out of academic options as a result of their behavior choices. School officials thought enough of these young people to create programs and employ speakers to motivate them toward higher ground. Following two speeches to this audience over the last couple of years, I come away with two thoughts. First, I was amazed at how bright so many of these young people are—and the only difference between them and "regular students" is the lack of accountability in their lives that can influence their decision-making. They hang out with the wrong people, make bad choices, and for the most part, live their lives however they choose.

> HAVE WE BECOME SO BUSY IN OUR PURSUIT OF THINGS THAT WE ARE GUILTY OF IGNORING THE MAIN THINGS?

The second observation is more disturbing. These young people are really no different than many of the students in "mainstream" school programs. Students are looking for someone who is genuine. They are looking for someone who is authentic. They are searching for a role model who has a high standard. These folks are not stupid. They are simply tired of the hypocrisy that exists in our society. They are tired of role models preaching a message they do not live.

On a scale of one to ten, with ten being the maximum, where would you rate your standard of excellence? Are you doing everything in your power to live a life of excellence? Aristotle said, "You are what you repeatedly do. Therefore, excellence ought to be a habit, not an act." In a superficial society of people who just want to make an impression, it takes far less energy and effort to make excellence an act. Thus, *appearing* excellent has become the acceptable societal norm. The problem is that those who choose to offer the appearance of excellence do not impact those around them. And the result is a culture of "at-risk" children. Look around you. They populate every strand of society—from grade school to college classrooms. Don't you think it's time to reconnect to the values of a generation of people who worried less about show and more about substance? Our children, our students, our employees, our leaders are in deep need of an alternative education—the kind of education that can only come from the timeless wisdom of a generation gone by.

Somehow we must issue a call to the elders of our communities to resume their rightful positions as guides. You can learn so much from someone who has been where you are trying to go. I recall when my wife passed away, the people who helped me the most were those who had walked a similar path. Oh how—to this very day—I depend on such wisdom that cannot come from any other source than walking through *the valley of the shadow of death.*

We need more people in our world who will tell it like it is. I would love to go to a graduation speech and hear a speaker say something like:

> You want to succeed? Follow the advice of Mark Twain who said, "I've never allowed my schooling to get in the way of my education." So graduates, today your formal education begins! Here's your first lesson. Find a wise mentor. The mentor must have endured some setbacks, failures, and disappointments—for wisdom rarely is acquired without a storm. Remain with this person for as long as you can. Learn, grow, and prosper!

I have found that when your back is to the wall you will decide to sit or stand! A former colleague on our A&M football coaching staff used to say, "If you want to know what's inside a man, just shake him up."

It has been said that with each generation the bar of excellence slips downward. I have discovered after two decades of teaching on the university level that most of my students—though awesome people—seem interested in doing a good job up to a point. I firmly believe that most *want* to do a good job as long as the price is not too steep. Just listen to the "student speak" a professor might endure in the course of a semester:

- What do I need to do to get a "C"?
- Is your class really hard?
- Will there be tests?
- Will I have to write a term paper?
- When is the deadline for dropping your course?

Before you begin bemoaning young people and the poor choices they make, consider statements echoed in buildings throughout the corridors of America's business community:

- I'm just here until something better comes along.
- Whether I work or sit, I still get the same pay.
- I'm not making waves—I'm not rocking the boat.
- I'm just buying time.
- I'll deal with it because of my retirement.
- It's just a job. Lose this one, get another one.

Examine these statements closely. What are young people saying about effort? What are workers saying about the value of hard work? The value of excellence? The value of doing a good job? Apparently, the goal no longer is to do the kind of work where one takes pride in the job. The goal no longer is to give maximum effort—the goal today seems to be the opposite of what legendary football coach Vince Lombardi once stressed.

Lombardi's love affair with and passion for the maximum pursuit of excellence was not developed during his illustrious coaching days with the Green Bay Packers, nor during a stellar career at Fordham University, where he along with six other linemen gained legendary fame as the "Seven Blocks of Granite." Lombardi discovered the great joy of pursuing excellence while playing football at St. Francis Prep School—at the time the oldest Catholic school in Brooklyn, New York. According to David Maraniss, it was after a prep school football game when Lombardi realized where the joy of pursuing excellence comes from:

> But the most telling moment of the season for Vinnie came at the conclusion of an early game against powerful Erasmus Hall, a public high school then in the midst of a long winning streak. Led by the golden arm of its crackerjack quarterback, Sid Luckman, Erasmus shut out St. Francis 13–0. Yet Lombardi, who smacked Luckman with a few good licks on defense, felt like anything but a loser when it was over. He experienced

what he later described as a locker room epiphany. As he sat slumped on the bench in his grass-stained red and blue uniform, he was overcome by joy, a rare feeling for him. Nothing on the sandlots felt quite like this. He understood that he was not a great player, but he had fought hard, given his best and discovered that no one on the field intimidated him, no matter how big or fast. He was confident, convinced that he could compete, puzzled why other players did not put out as much as he had. He felt fatigue, soreness, competitive yearning, accomplishment—and all of this, he said later, left him surprisingly elated.[13]

There is a timeless value reflected in the life of Vince Lombardi that needs to permeate our present culture. Whatever happened to taking pride in doing a good job? Whatever happened to the joy that comes from knowing you have done your best? Do you take pride in what you do? How would your career change if you made a decision to find joy in the process of doing good work? Ours is a society that has become so outcome-oriented that the joy of the process often escapes. Vince Lombardi—during a locker room epiphany—offers a simple lesson that can inspire a greater degree of excellence in our lives!

Whether you're a CEO, educator, or student, you can no longer afford to live a life devoid of excellence. Earlier sentiments shared by students offer but a glimpse of an educational divide of epidemic proportion. As news sources bombard us with stories chronicling the deterioration of our educational system, the rapidly declining literacy rate, and the soaring numbers of teachers leaving the ranks,[14] we realize that we are quickly evolving into a society polarized not merely along ethnic, economic, political, or religious dimensions, but along the corridors of intelligence that once anchored a new generation to the wisdom, insight, and understanding of those who preceded them. It is a kind of wisdom that offers a type of work ethic whereby the paycheck and benefits package is not viewed as the primary motivation for excelling. It is a kind of wisdom that caused one to approach work with gratitude and humility—grateful for an opportunity to be employed. It is a kind of wisdom that produced employees who viewed honest and hard work—regardless of assignment or position—as both honorable and noble.

My father's generation epitomized people who valued working hard and took pride in doing things the correct way. As you think about this era of worker, several distinguishable qualities are worth noting. Such are the attributes that produce marketplace greatness and are worthy of a renaissance in our modern era. Specifically, these attributes can be reduced to two basics for excellence: listening and learning.

LISTENING

There is no coincidence that greatness usually follows a disciplined approach to living out one's life with skill. Not surprisingly, a defining characteristic of people who live at such a level is an absolute commitment to the discipline of listening. As one who has taught communication-related courses on the university level for over twenty years, I am confident in the assertion that there is a clear distinction between hearing and listening. Hearing is an automatic process that occurs rather naturally. Thus, the process of hearing is passive at best. Hearing requires no skill sets, knowledge base, or special training. We *hear* messages while the television is on, while the shower is running, and while we are multi-tasking. Is there any wonder why we miss so much content? I like the quote, "Hearing tells you the music is playing. Listening tells you what the song is saying!"

Basic communication theory suggests two levels of communication: the content level and the relational level. On the content level, the actual meaning of the message is communicated. Conversely, the relational level reveals the power positions of those speaking—subordinates and superiors—and establishes who is in control and who is not. When we *hear*, we fail to comprehend, categorize, or control most of the content. What we hear are the relational tones, which may or may not accurately represent the message.

Listening, on the other hand, is the active process of gathering, storing, and utilizing messages. Active listening involves thinking, filtering, assimilating, paraphrasing, focusing, retaining, and responding. Active listening is both verbal and nonverbal. People who practice active listening skills are at a significant advantage in the workplace and in relationships. What chance is there of catching wisdom if you are always talking? There was a sign in my parents' bedroom that read, "A fish would not get caught if he kept his mouth shut!" You might be amazed at how much you learn by just being quiet and listening more than being loud and talking. Note the tangible characteristics of wise people:

- They are slow to talk.
- They are quick to listen.
- They are always thinking.
- They evaluate every message.
- Their response is measured and thoughtful.
- They are wordsmiths; they do not waste words.

- They do not talk to be heard.
- They do not speak to impress.
- They use words when absolutely necessary.
- They use words to reveal knowledge.
- They use words to elevate understanding.
- Their primary goal is to be understood.
- Their secondary goal is to share information.

I just described Roger Marion Rigsby—a third-grade dropout with a world-class fountain of wisdom. How so? At some point in his life, Dad learned that the key to getting ahead was found in actively listening. Maybe he developed the habit of good listening while growing up in the country communities surrounding Huntsville, Texas. Or did he use the strategy of active listening to offset not being able to read and write as a child? Or did listening become his greatest ally during his Army years? Or did he realize that a deficit in his formal education would require expert listening as he performed his duties as a cook at California Maritime Academy? The intimidation of learning new cultures in ports of call as varied as the Philippines and Panama would require more than basic skill sets to overcome.

My father was a master listener. Construct a list of genuinely good people—people from every walk of life who are distinguished not by salary or position or possession but by a sheer desire to be their best. They share common characteristics of persistence, determination, vision, and the pursuit of excellence. And at the foundation of these individuals is an acute appreciation for and love of listening. They have learned that taking in information creates advantage, opportunity, promotion, wealth, and wisdom.

My father, whether forced by circumstances or as the result of his personality, was a steadfast listener. He would rather listen than speak. He was the quietest one in our family. When he talked, his words were not wasted. But his was a vocation of listening. He got it. Dad realized that listening was more advantageous than talking. He was never without wisdom. Wisdom was Dad's friend, his constant companion. And in retrospect, his desire and ability to listen to others produced an unusual skill set of intellect and common sense. Listening was the essence of who my father was.

LEARNING

Maybe it's just me. But as a college professor, I have noticed with increasing regularity that many students do not attend a university to learn. In my two decades as a university level instructor, I have found that most students—certainly not all—attend the university for a *degree* rather than an education! The great casualty in academia is learning! We have reared a generation of incredibly bright young people, who have been fed a diet of instant gratification, seasoned with self-absorbed heroes who function in a culture that encourages superficiality.

Television has taught us that life is easy, fun, and without consequences for quitting. More devastating is the mediated message that you really do not have to work hard. Rather offer the appearance of hard work. Many students are crippled further by parents who pamper and praise rather than challenge and charge their child to stand and learn in the midst of tough times. Filled with mixed signals and pressures to land a "dream job" in four years, students survey the landscape, learn from their campus elders, pick professors based on ease and popularity, and waste countless opportunities to develop a breadth and depth that might well serve them for a lifetime. Their goal is not learning from the process of education, but learning how to play the academic game. They spend four or five years following the well-traveled paths of the academic maze. With supporters cheering such sentiments as, "just get your degree;" "buckle down and get through class;" "just write the paper and turn it in," is there any wonder why so many CEOs are finding it increasingly more difficult to recruit from colleges?

Conversely, consider the malaise of mediocrity in the

workplace today! Author John Mason was right on target when he titled his book, *An Enemy Called Average*.[15]

There is a plausible link between one's desire to learn and the level of excellence attained. Allowing schooling to interrupt education is commonplace today. When the institution becomes paramount over the learning, a casualty will be excellence.

But do not think that it's just in the classroom. Recently some top-level executives were discussing major problems within their company. As an invited speaker, I arrived early and learned a great deal from observing a leadership roundtable discussion. The most startling insight came from one of the vice presidents who said in a direct and succinct manner, "Our problem is we have placed systems over people." Great technology does not necessarily compute to great companies. Our parents understood this. Perhaps we ought to rethink our values.

Lessons from my father sustain me in every endeavor— whether on the football field or in the pulpit, I depend on the wisdom I learned from my parents, especially my father. "Son, if you're not going to do it right, it's not worth doing at all." Those words ring with a piercing familiarity in a society that would rather look good than do good.

My father simply believed in doing your best. Implicit here is a focus on process. If I could collect my Dad's wisdom regarding excellence and offer it in one sentence, it would be this: *focus on doing your very best right now, and don't stop!* The primary goal is not to finish first. The primary goal is not to get the top grade. The primary goal is to do your best. Talk to any football coach; they will tell you effort is more important than results. Talk to any leader or supervisor; they will tell you effort consistently is more important than results.

Mike Clark is among the best strength coaches in America. While he was on our staff at Texas A&M, he won the NCAA Strength Coach of the Year twice. As head strength coach for the Seattle Seahawks—a team that went to its first Super Bowl in 2006—Clark was named the 2005 NFL's Strength Coach of the Year. In the decade that I have known Coach Clark, he has preached to players constantly that effort is far more important than talent:

You show me any athlete at any level who gives maximum effort, and I will show you a player who will excel. It is not a matter of talent. It's not a question of where you went in the draft. The question is do you have the heart of a champion? And at the heart of every champion I have ever coached is a dedicated effort to be the absolute best you can be. Results are important. But results don't define who you are as a man. Success is not being a first-round draft pick. Success is using your God-given ability to give maximum effort every day—whether you're in the NFL, teach school, or work construction.

Results are critical, but are very predictable if you do not give maximum effort!

In our outcome-oriented culture, the emphasis is on the bottom line. Rewards are bestowed upon those who finish first. Value is assigned to those who get top marks. Let me make this very clear: I would rather my students get "C" level grades with 100 percent effort than receive "A" marks without the struggle necessary in the process of improvement. And when students come along with that type of mentality, they are distinguished among the student body.

One such example is former Texas A&M and NFL star Dat Nguyen. This young man gives maximum effort to everything he does, and as a result, good things come to him. The only Vietnamese-born person to play football in the NFL (linebacker with the Dallas Cowboys) came to Texas A&M as an overweight freshman, reluctantly accepted a red shirt his freshman year, and left five years later as an All-American linebacker with 517 tackles— more tackles than anyone in A&M history!

Physically, Dat is not the typical NFL linebacker (5'11", 238 pounds), but his heart cannot be measured. I watched this young man give his very best every down of every quarter of every game. When you give that kind of effort, size becomes a moot issue. Winner of the Chuck Bednarik Award as College Football's Defensive Player of the Year in 1998, Dat continues to excel in the NFL because of an explosive work ethic that pushes him to give maximum effort every day.

Maybe it was rising to overcome the challenges of his red-shirt year. Maybe it was something his parents planted inside him. Whatever motivated Dat Nguyen, his story exceeds the parameters of stardom on the gridiron. Born in a refugee camp, Dat and his family fled Vietnam after the fall of Saigon in 1975. The family settled in Rockport, Texas, where Dat eventually played football in high school, compiling 188 tackles and was named a Consensus Texas Top 100 linebacker. But to hear Dat talk, it's not about the records or the stats: "It's a huge step for the Vietnamese community to have a Vietnamese football player. That's why I don't worry about expectations. To me, I walked the mile. I play for the love of the game."[16]

If you did not know any better, you would think Dat Nguyen is from a different generation. He's a throwback to a generation of people who took pride in what they did. He reflects a generation that did a good job because they were supposed to do a good job. He's a throwback to an era of athletes who played the game for the love of playing the game. Clearly, the emerging great divide in our world today is between those who excel and those who go through the motions—between what I refer to as doers and viewers. Which are you?

What is the great problem with wanting to do good work? Why is our era obsessed with the notion of just getting by? Why is there no longer any pride in what we do? As I consider wisdom revealed in the life of the wisest man I've ever met, I realize some answers to my questions.

Roger Rigsby believed the worth of an individual was found in keeping his word, treating people kindly, and doing your best. He simply and unwittingly lived this life every day. No fanfare. No limelight. No need or desire for acclaim. My father—like the fathers of his generation— believed they were doing nothing particularly special. They were doing what they had been taught—to play the man.[17]

The work ethic of my father's generation reveals honor, strength of character, and a sense of pride for a job well done. The focus of the work was on the excellence of the work. The worker paid dutiful attention to details encountered during the process of a task. A good job meant attention to every detail. Legendary football coach Joe Paterno once said, "If you do the little things right, the big things will take care of themselves."[18] The worker took pride in striving for excellence and worked diligently to accomplish the best results. During his induction speech into Major League Baseball's Hall of Fame, Ozzie Smith shared a quote that guided his success on the field:

Good enough is not good enough if it can be better.
And better is not good enough if it can be best.

This quote not only serves as an outstanding challenge to mediocrity, but it reveals a clear contrast of how work is valued between two generations. Ozzie Smith did not lower his effort to match the expectations of his critics. Do you perform to meet the expectations of others? Or are your expectations so high that mediocrity is not even in your vocabulary?

The work ethic of our generation does not reveal honor, strength of character, and a sense of pride for a job well done. Rather, our present value system is contingent upon looking smart and appearing righteous. Strength of image and pride in self are tantamount to a healthy being—the aesthetic ethic for the new millennium employee. The focus of our work is to finish—and to look good finishing the task. There is little concern for honor, no need for excellence, and no tangible benefit in revealing one's true character.

If there is to be a revival of excellence today, there first must be a willingness to reconnect to a value—a wisdom from a generation of people who were averse to spotlights and image consultants, and who stood firm in their desire to put forth maximum effort in their pursuit of excellence.

GOOD ENOUGH IS NOT GOOD ENOUGH IF IT CAN BE BETTER. AND BETTER IS NOT GOOD ENOUGH IF IT CAN BE BEST.

"Son, if you're going to do a job, do it right." Dad, I get it. You were not talking about a specific task as much as you were attempting to establish a mindset—a fortified commitment to be your best in every way, to do your best every day, and to give your best with little to say. Excellence thus becomes the sole requirement for total satisfaction. And once we taste excellence as habit rather than act, we will never be satisfied with the stale bread of mediocrity and the sour juice of image promotion.

In thinking about my own struggles with excellence, I have observed college students and workers at every level facing similar challenges. I have come to the conclusion that our outcome-oriented way of doing things may be more of a culprit that robs us of excellence than we might think.

My father never rushed. Never. He took his time and paid tremendous attention to every single detail. He focused on each segment of every stage of the process. In essence, Dad learned that the secret of success was found in the joy of doing your best one step at a time. The lesson here reinforces Coach Paterno's belief that attention to and focus on the little things can have huge results.

The work of Malcolm Gladwell has helped my thinking tremendously in this area. In Gladwell's national bestseller, *The Tipping Point,* the author talks about how small things can make the greatest difference.

In an effort to understand a *Tipping Point*—that moment in time that starts an epidemic or a social phenomenon—Gladwell deconstructs the epidemic cycle and characterizes its salient features. Whether discussing the spread of a disease, a decrease in urban crime rates, or the rise of a clothing fad, Gladwell identifies the features that create the phenomena—and thus he is able to isolate the approximate point when activity makes a dramatic change:

> These three characteristics—one, contagiousness; two, the fact that little causes can have big effects; and three, that change happens not gradually but at one dramatic moment—are the same three principles that define how measles move through a grade-school classroom or the flu attacks every winter. Of the three, the third trait— the idea that epidemics can rise or fall in one dramatic moment—is the most important, because it is the principle that makes sense of the first two and that permits

the greatest insight into why modern change happens the way it does. The name given to that one dramatic moment in an epidemic when everything can change all at once is the Tipping Point.[19]

Is success eluding you because you are not paying attention to the little things? Do you have your eye on the big picture or the bottom line, and not on the fact that the big picture and the bottom line are constructed with painstaking effort?

Maybe it's time to slow down and get better. Maybe the goal is not to study harder but to study smarter! Maybe the goal in leadership is to shift from a singular focus on the bottom line to integrating excellence in processes and protocols along the journey.

How would your leadership change if you became more of a process-oriented leader? What changes would your report card reveal if you began taking fewer notes, and actually listened more to what was being said? How much faster would you climb the corporate ladder if you began focusing on excellence and maximum effort in the process and not just the end result?

Maybe we ought to slow down and quiet ourselves for a while; at least long enough to listen to some of that wisdom from a generation gone by.

CHAPTER 6

LESSONS ON CHARACTER

CHARACTER IS WHAT YOU DO . . . IN THE DARK

—DWIGHT L. MOODY

Of all Dad's virtues, none was revealed more prominently than character. Roger Marion Rigsby epitomized character. He lived character. His very essence was character. My father believed to the core of his being that a man was not worth much if he could not be trusted to do the right thing at the right time in the right way. Just listen to the rhetoric that shaped my reality on the topic of character:

- Son, if a man will lie to you, he'll steal from you.
- Son, always tell the truth. A lying tongue cannot be defended.
- Son, always do the right thing. Always!
- Son, if you tell a man you're going to do something, do it!

- Son, the only thing you own is your name.
  Protect its honor.
- Son, learn to do your best. Always!
- Son, a good reputation is worth more than riches.
- Son, protect your reputation.
- Son, mean what you say and say what you mean.
- Son, always treat people with respect.
- Son, most of all, respect yourself and others will respect you.
- Son, never take anything that does not belong to you.
- Son, learn to close your mouth and listen.
- Son, love your family more than your job.
- Son, honor the Lord in everything you do.

Sometimes I think my father could have written Proverbs! He was *that* wise. I use a portion of his wisdom every day of my life. My father's wisdom has been my roadmap through unspeakable joys and unimaginable lows. During my tenure as a television news reporter, it was my father's wisdom which instructed me that the great stories are developed as reporters close their mouths and open their ears.

Through graduate school, my father's wisdom taught me to be a man of my word, regardless of the cost. As a college professor, my father's wisdom beckoned me to be just as respectful to the janitor who cleaned as I would be to the university president who governed. As a minister and motivational speaker, my father's life of character speaks bold pronouncements from the grave—as he walks with me day by day telling me to live a life that is blameless, upright, God-fearing, and evil-resisting (Job 1:1). Thank you, Dad. Thank you for not worrying about being popular with your children. A popular father would assist me little in a world that invites inhabitants to barter their character.

Pastor Andy Stanley once defined character as an absolute belief in right and wrong, and choosing right regardless of the cost. My father simply and unwittingly chose to do the right thing the right way all the time. There was no gray area when it came to Roger Rigsby and doing the right thing. Today's business leaders could learn something from this simple man from Huntsville, Texas! The essence of his day was character. And not surprisingly, every other trait—excellence, loyalty, kindness, helpfulness—all were born out of his heart of character. Just think about this for a moment. Think about the power you have when you endorse a life of character. Think about the opportunities to help others. Think about the chances to develop meaningful relationships. Think about the increasing number of meaningful conversations. Just think how different your life would be if you lived with the ultimate goal of being your best every single day. Consider the possible outcomes:

- Dependability
- Loyalty
- Trustworthiness
- Excellence
- Appropriateness
- Determinedness
- Persistence
- Wisdom
- Sound judgment
- Caring
- Kindness
- Honesty

Now, ask yourself this question. How many people—among your circle of relatives, friends, and co-workers—possess several of these qualities? Write their names down. I would be willing to assume that you wrote very few names on your sheet of paper. Why? Because we live in a culture that encourages our "essence" to reveal strength of image rather than strength of character. What we do in the dark remains in the dark. Modern translation: What we do in Las Vegas stays in Las Vegas.

Such sentiments have become a culture's acceptable

code of morality—a morality that hints of deception and allows for tolerance. What's the result? A culture with no social responsibility to speak truthfully. Families would rather be entertained by the pirates of pop culture than confronted by timeless wisdom. A generation of people would rather bask in visual success than stand steadfast on concrete conventions. In a nutshell, we are going to the dogs.

Howard Hendricks said it best when he asserted, "The greatest crisis in America today is a crisis of leadership. And the greatest peril of leadership is a crisis of character."[20]

Should character continue its absence from the landscape of American culture, I question the strength of our technological supremacy or the fortitude of our nuclear family. I doubt seriously whether a culture, company, team, ministry, or family can endure hardship or celebrate success without a foundation of character. If there is anything missing from society today that has the potential to restore families, resurrect careers, and revive corporate settings, the resilient manifestation of authentic character is that transformative agent of change—one desperately needed in our new millennium society of interactive relationships and techno-supported conversations. Technology is not the issue here. The lack of authentic character is. So, what does authentic character look like?

THE FACE OF AUTHENTIC CHARACTER

In two decades of teaching at the university level, I taught thousands of students—lots of gifted young people with great promise. Most followed instructions and put forth good effort in a genuine spirit of academic accomplishment. Most of the students did reasonably well with a few exceptions at either end of the grading spectrum. Here's the point. Among the thousands of students taught, only a handful displayed sincere character. Let me help you to see what character is by illustrating what character is not through the words of good-hearted, well-meaning young people:

- Never assume responsibility for actions.
- Test failure does not mean that the student failed. Test failure means that the material the student chose to focus on did not match information on the exam!

Additionally, I was always fascinated by how many computer printers choose to "crash" the day an assigned paper was due.

- It's the printer's fault!

- The disk was infected!
- The paper jammed!

Never—in twenty years—did I hear a student remark, "I waited until the last minute to begin this process. My lack of discipline and my inability to budget time properly resulted in little margin for error!"

Before you climb on the bandwagon of those who have few positive things to say about college students, consider this. A failure to assume responsibility is epidemic and not exclusive to campus life. In fact, the students learned those skillful responses somewhere! Most adults you encounter have difficulty assuming responsibility for actions. Is this a spiritual issue, political problem, or social dilemma? No, this is a character issue. Character assumes the proper behavior at all times. Webster's Dictionary defines character as moral strength, self-discipline, and fortitude. Simply stated, character wills the heart and charges the tongue to speak truth regardless of circumstances (moral strength). Character demands that one's will be motivated by a finely tuned set of values based on a moral standard, and you adhere to that standard

> SIMPLY STATED, CHARACTER WILLS THE HEART AND CHARGES THE TONGUE TO SPEAK TRUTH REGARDLESS OF CIRCUMSTANCES (MORAL STRENGTH).

regardless of feelings, emotions, or past experiences (self-discipline). Character establishes irrevocable patterns for your life whereby you instinctively choose right—regardless of the cost!

A very good read is the book *Yeager*, the autobiography of test pilot Chuck Yeager. I was most intrigued by his description of the flight, which resulted in him flying faster than the speed of sound: "I was accelerating at 31 mph per second, approaching 1,650 mph, the fastest any pilot had yet flown and the fastest that any straight-winged airplane would ever fly." At this point, Yeager was traveling Mach 2.4—over two times the speed of sound. His altitude was 80,000 feet. He was flying too high and too fast:

> The wing kept coming up and I was powerless to keep from rolling over. And then we started going in four different directions at once, careening all over the sky, snapping and rolling and spinning in what pilots call going divergent on all three axes. I called it hell. I was crashing around in that cockpit, slamming violently from side to side, front to back, battered to the point where I was too stunned to think. Terrifying. The thought flashed: I lost my tail. I've had it. G-forces yanked me upwards with such force that my helmet cracked the canopy. Without my seat straps, I probably would've been blasted right through the glass. My

pressure suit suddenly inflated with a loud hiss. I was gasping and my face plate fogged. Blinded, being pounded to death, I wondered where in the Sierras I was about to drill a hole.[21]

As the plane went into a downward spin, he thought it was all over. Dramatically he was able to regain control at 25,000 feet and land on the lakebed of California's Mojave Desert. Reading his data, Yeager realized that he had dropped 51,000 feet in 51 seconds. He credits his survival to "sheer instinct and pure luck." Yeager explains that he had practiced and worked so diligently in the weeks and months prior to the test flight that his instincts took over—even when he was too stunned to react. Yeager *instinctively* knew what to do to regain control.

Making right choices every day may seem insignificant. You may ask, "What's the point? No one will ever know my choice or my decision." However, what we learn from General Yeager is that those daily choices have the power to instruct your instincts to remain in control—even when everything around you is out of control.

> THOSE DAILY CHOICES HAVE THE POWER TO INSTRUCT YOUR INSTINCTS TO REMAIN IN CONTROL—EVEN WHEN EVERYTHING AROUND YOU IS OUT OF CONTROL.

How different would your life look if you . . . ? Each one of us is going to be in our very own cockpit experience at 80,000 feet, flying 1,650 miles per hour, and spinning out of control. It may not be a test flight, but a financial difficulty, inescapable tension on the job, or even the death of a family member. How are you going to handle that situation? What you do this very day will instruct your instincts to either soar to the highest level of character, or crash emotionally, physically, and spiritually.

How about living in such a way that the positive character choices you make work to instruct your instincts moment by moment, day by day, month by month, and year by year? It is entirely possible and quite achievable to make such powerful choices that your life will instinctively choose that which is right regardless of the cost. Such an authentic life looks something like this:

- I admit fault without hesitation.
- I assume responsibility for my actions.
- I speak 100 percent truth 100 percent of the time.
- If I don't know it, I don't speak it.
- If I don't believe it, I don't speak it.
- If I don't practice it, I don't speak it.
- If I say I'm going to do something, I do it.
- I don't lie, cheat, or steal.

- I operate with sound judgment and am not given to exaggeration.
- My conduct is circumspect.
- My behavior is consistent in all situations.
- I treat people with the utmost respect.
- I am slow to anger.
- I am not easily discouraged.
- I help whenever and wherever possible.
- I have great passion for living life.
- I am loyal.
- I listen well.
- I honor people by being genuinely interested in them.
- I hold a confidence.
- I do not talk about another.
- I never say anything bad about anyone.
- I am kind to everyone.
- My countenance is cheerful.
- My spirit is joyful.

This was my father! I have never met anyone like him. He simply lived character. His impact was astronomical. I thank God that I have such a legacy to follow, emulate, and build upon. My father was a good man. There is so much in that statement—a good man. Read these words from my good friend, bestselling author, speaker, and national radio host Dr. Gary Rosberg:

> A few years ago, during the coldest night of my life (minus 23 degrees), my mother and I stood at the bedside of my dying father at a hospital near Lambeau Field in Green Bay, Wisconsin. After Dad slipped into the arms of Jesus, my mother looked into my eyes and said, "Your dad was a good man. He was a loving man, an honest, and a good man." At that moment, I realized what else is there to be in life but a good man.[22]

The poignancy of that phrase hit me so hard that I dedicated the rest of my life to living in such a way that my four boys will someday say, "Our dad was a good man." Rosberg noted that his mother did not say his father was a great man, but rather a good man. His father—like mine—was not perfect, made mistakes, had shortcomings, did things he probably regretted, but through it all he was tabbed with the label, "a good man."

What greater standard than to have family and friends approve your conduct as good. After all is said and done, what really is the measure or worth of a person's life? Accomplishments are important, and possessions have value. But honors and materials do not represent what you stand for, who you are, or even how you will be remembered.

I recall a statement I heard former Texas A&M head football Coach R.C. Slocum say dozens of times:

> My value as a head football coach will not be based on how many football games I won or lost. My value will be directly related to the quality of the lives of the men I coached. Are my former players productive citizens, good employees, good husbands and fathers? The quality of their lives is the standard by which I will be judged as a head coach.[23]

I recently heard Coach Slocum offer this very same remark. The venue was the induction ceremony for the Texas Sports Hall of Fame, Class of 2005. Once again, in front of hundreds of guests including many former players, he told the audience that his greatest legacy is in the work and lives of his former players. Are they good men, good husbands, and good fathers? Are they productive members of society who handle their affairs with integrity—their triumphs with humility and their defeats with dignity?

I have spent many hours visiting with Coach Slocum about this very topic. Winning football games was a high priority. Developing men of character was even higher. I recall so many times visiting with staff members such as Tim Cassidy, former Director of Football Operations, and former coaches such as Steve Kragthorpe, Ken Rucker, Mike Sherman, Mike Hankwitz, Buddy Wyatt, Ray Dorr, Alan Waddell, and so many others who regarded character development in players as a high priority.

Regardless of accomplishments, successes, wins, losses, championships, rings, salaries, and status, for Coach Slocum, character was paramount. As a member of his staff for six years, I witnessed Coach Slocum demanding his coaches be men of character and insisting that his players mirror the same. We had hundreds of talks about ways to challenge, stimulate, and encourage character development among our student athletes. Since 2002, I have been most fortunate to serve current Aggie head football coach Dennis Franchione as team chaplain. Coach Fran has developed a strong player leadership council and character courses for football players. Current coaches make a committed effort to model that character before the players.

The lessons learned during those important years have the potential to help you in business, education, and life. Consider the following lessons learned from a decade of observing Division One football from the inside:

- Character is transferable. I noted that if a young man displayed character off the field, he was likely to make the right choices on the field. Consider the words of current University of Tulsa head coach Steve Kragthorpe: "There is an undeniable correlation between on-and off-the-field behavior. If a player takes care of his business off the field, he is more than likely going to do the right things on the field. He will run the precise route; he will block in the proper scheme; he will be in the right coverage. There is no question that character is transferable."

- Character reveals itself in private as well as in public. Former Texas A&M and NFL running back Rodney Thomas was the epitome of character. One of my favorite stories is of Thomas observing fellow players in the residence hall banging the vending machine in an effort to free the soft drink cans without paying. After the damage was done and the coast was clear, someone observed Thomas replenishing the vending machine with quarters. That—as Dwight L. Moody might say—is character in the dark!

- Character demands respect. Among the greatest individuals I have encountered is the late Ray Dorr, former quarterbacks' coach for A&M. The impact he had on the lives of players and coaches—in health as well as sickness—defies description. Ray Dorr was an inspiration to all who knew him. And because of his character—even in the midst of suffering from Amyotrophic Lateral Sclerosis (ALS, also known as Lou Gehrig's disease)—his impact will be felt for generations to come.

- Character keeps you on the right path. College basketball coaching legend Mike Krzyzewski tells the story of his mother insisting that he get on the right bus. The phrase reminded him that even if his tendency was to head the wrong way, be with people going the right way! The vast majority of our players—past and present—stayed the course. They remained on the right path. This is not the stuff that sells newspapers and boosts talk show ratings, but it is the stuff that builds a solid foundation for living a life of influence, a life that makes an impact rather than an impression!

Living a lifestyle of character means you are choosing right regardless of the cost, regardless of the consequences, and regardless of the circumstances. Such a life leaves a legacy for eternity. Such a life makes an impact and not merely an impression. Note well that such a lifestyle comes with high requirements. You must be sold on living well. Isn't it interesting that we make great effort to travel well, work well, play well, and even eat well? How about a steadfast commitment to living well?

In the world of business, character is the "hot" topic

today. You cannot go through one day without hearing about the antics of someone who has violated a trust in one way or another. And many corporations are responding by changing hiring practices, implementing more stringent policies, hiring consultants and behavior gurus, and enforcing mandatory character training for employees.

A major step toward the institutional implication of policy resulted when Congress passed the Sarbanes-Oxley Act of 2002—a move that compels companies to consider and remain mindful of the ethical dimensions of doing business.[24] Mark Pyatt, a global marketing strategist with SAP Labs, LLC, argues that Sarbanes-Oxley reinforces a moral ethic desperately absent in business practices today:

> "Sarbanes-Oxley brings an ethical reality back into the mainstream of business. The act puts in place a type of moral checks and balances for corporations— something that should have been there all along. The result of this congressional act is that it is forcing companies to deal with character issues in a way that holds people accountable from the top to the bottom of the organizational chart."[25]

Are you ready to commit to a life that makes an impact? Why not take stock of your life right now? I want you to respond to the following questions on this page. You won't need to tabulate your score with a numerical system to determine your character. You will see what you already know—in black and white! Pause for a moment and do a little personal inventory by responding to the following questions:

- Are people drawn to your authenticity? (Are you real?)
- Are you a joy to be around (positive or negative)?
- Is your behavior so consistent that your responses are predictable?
- Are your responses to triumph and adversity identical?
- Is there total consistency between what you say and do?
- Is your life transparent (no secret life)?
- Do you protect confidential conversations?
- Do you apologize quickly?
- Are you fast to forgive?
- Does it take a lot to discourage you?
- Are your decisions based on core values (rather than emotions or feelings)?
- Are you positive by nature?
- Do you speak positively about others?
- Are you reluctant to complain?

- Is there a willingness to see the big picture (is your vision impaired)?
- Is there a willingness to help others?
- Are you reluctant to quit or give up?
- Is your tendency to be an overcomer rather than a victim?
- Do you remain silent if you have nothing positive or constructive to share?
- Do you encourage and uplift people around you?
- Are you a kind person?
- Do you say "Thank you" regularly?
- Do you have a genuine desire to help others?
- Are your motives under constant evaluation?
- Are you generally more concerned about the welfare of others?
- Are you willing to communicate during relational turmoil (arguments!)?
- Do you honor the other person during arguments?
- Do you honor people in your actions as well as words?
- Are you early or at least on time for commitments?
- Do you listen actively (rather than *hearing passively*)?
- Do you look people directly in the eyes when you talk to them?

- Do you keep your word when you say something?
- Are you honest in every situation or circumstance?
- Do you tell the truth when you play golf?
- Do you tell the truth when you file your taxes?
- Do you tell the truth about spending money?
- Do you tell the truth about your weight or your age?
- Are your words forthright and straightforward?
- Have you overcome the temptation to exaggerate or embellish?
- Have you stopped dropping names?
- Do you end conversations when gossip and rumor become apparent?
- Do you practice common decency?
- Do you live your convictions every day?
- Are you growing in wisdom every day?
- Do you surround yourself with people smarter and wiser than you?
- Do people approach you because they know you offer sound wisdom?
- Do your actions and words reveal humility over exaltation?
- Are you willing to pursue excellence regardless of attainment?
- Have you overcome the insatiable desire to be popular?

- Have you moved beyond living for the approval of others?

- Is it more important to you to be righteous rather than right?

- Do you go to bed every night with a clean heart and a clear conscious?

If you said "yes" to most of these statements, you are making an impact in your world. You are changing your environment for the better! You are what the late T. W. Wilson would refer to as a person who possesses "next-level influence."

Here's your opportunity for greatness. I want you take inventory of your character and place it where you can study it every day for one year! I realize a habit requires repetition for at least thirty days; however, I am not talking about developing a single habit. I want you to establish a new way of life! And daily reminders are the very first step, for they help you become aware of what you are doing right and changes you need to address. If you continue to live your life in the fog of denial, you'll never realize that others need help! Furthermore, the fog has the power to shroud you from the realization that you have been given this gift called life, and you can make choices to minimize your influence by living a superficial and artificial life, or you can choose to live a passionate life fueled by authentic character that maximizes your influences and builds a legacy for generations to come. If you choose to make a commitment to living well—to making choices that reflect the highest degree of character and integrity—instinctively you will live in a different dimension than most. You will begin to experience unbridled joy, unspeakable peace, undeniable pleasure, and overwhelming satisfaction that all come with living well!

Are you ready to change your environment?

CHAPTER 7

STAND!

NEVER, NEVER, NEVER, NEVER GIVE UP!

—SIR WINSTON CHURCHILL

This book began as I stood at my wife's casket. Flanked by two young sons and a host of relatives and friends, our lives were over, our dreams dashed, our future bleak. I don't know if you ever had a life-altering moment, but it is rather surreal. I felt as though I was watching someone else in a horror movie. This couldn't be me! This could not be my life! Not the kid whose mother told him he was special so many times that he actually believed it. Not the young man who married his college sweetheart! Not the college intern who got the television gig before he graduated! Yes, my life was charmed—a fairy tale!

Trina LaFaye Williams was a beautiful young nursing student in her second year at California State University, Chico when we met in 1974. I fell in love at first sight. So did every other guy on campus! We began dating and eventually started "going steady"—a term about as odd-sounding these days as picture-tube television or Betamax recorders. We eventually graduated from college, began our careers, married, and started a family.

Trina was a labor and delivery nurse at a nearby hospital. I was learning all about the world of *impression* at our local CBS affiliate. I was grateful for the opportunity of a lifetime to enter my chosen profession, and I always will be appreciative to KHSL Television in Chico, California, for giving an untested rookie a chance. I had entered the world of television, and my ego soared!

It's been said that, "Ego is the anesthesia that deadens the pain of stupidity." My ego retarded my growth, stunted my development, and resulted in my living superficially for quite some time. But deep inside, those lessons I had learned from my father were there. And when that fast-paced, sometimes bizarre world of television was about to claim another victim, I began hearing my father's words with a piercing familiarity.

Television news is one of the most exciting fields imaginable. There are never two days that are exactly the same. One day, you are discussing budget issues with a city council member. The next day you are covering a freak spring blizzard at Mt. Shasta. And the next day you are interviewing screen legend Burt Reynolds, who is in town shooting his new movie. There is no such thing as "routine" in television news. You begin your career at 200 miles per hour, and you end your career at 200 miles per hour!

I always admired the people I worked with who were able to function in such a crazy fishbowl, yet maintain a kind of humility and character that could impact others. Clearly, I was not among that group. At this stage in my life, making an impact was about the last thing on my mind. I'm on television, baby! I'm a local celebrity! Life is good! I'm a star! As I said, *ego is the anesthesia that deadens the pain of stupidity!*

As for Trina and me, our lives were great! We had awesome jobs, great friends, and a fantastic church with a dynamic pastor—Ray Shelton, a prince of a preacher and powerful role model in my life whom I still consider "my pastor." Eventually, Trina gave birth to two beautiful sons—Jeremiah Benjamin Rigsby, in 1982, and Andrew David Rigsby, in 1985.

EGO IS THE ANESTHESIA THAT DEADENS THE PAIN OF STUPIDITY!

We were living the American dream in a small northern California college town. Chico is one of the most beautiful little towns in all of America. It doesn't get much better than going to college, falling in love with your college sweetheart, getting married, landing your first gig in television, working with great people at the local CBS shop, and having a beautiful and intelligent spouse—who dedicated her professional life to assisting in the delivery of babies! Our lives were picture-perfect. Nights were spent falling in love all over again in each other's arms.

Weekends meant adventurous journeys throughout what we call the "north state" portion of California—from exploring Mount Shasta and picnicking at Mount Lassen, to fishing at Lake Almanor and camping at Burney Falls, to hiking the Feather River Canyon and snow skiing at nearby Lake Tahoe. Occasionally we made the three-hour trek south to San Francisco to watch the Giants or take in a show and have dinner. Sometimes we'd head a few hours west to enjoy Mendocino, a quaint Victorian village nestled amidst the redwoods on the California coast. Life was perfect. Picture-perfect.

Then, one simple visit to a doctor's office changed the course of our lives forever. The year 1990 represented new beginnings for my young family. I had just graduated with a Ph.D. from the University of Oregon. My wife held the house together during those lean years, and now we were ready to take on the world! Next stop—Fresno, California! I would teach at Fresno State during the week and occasionally speak at churches or Christian camps during the weekend. Our children were in elementary school, and we made friends fast in this great central California city.

The Lord always blessed us by connecting us to great

churches—and Fresno was at the top of the list. Valley Christian Center and Pastor Roger Witlow impacted me like few others. As a very young minister with no formal ministerial training, I was hungry to observe and learn. Pastor Roger was, in my opinion, the model of Christian leadership—humble, caring, devoted, and non-wavering in his commitment to preach Christ clearly. There was no *showboating* at Valley Christian Center. There were no *superstars* at Valley. You worshiped, received the Word of God, and left committed to change your life and the world. In just a few months, Pastor Roger would play a very important role in our lives.

We loved our "post-grad school" life! If Chico was central to many attractions, imagine living in Fresno—where you are just two hours away from three national parks (Yosemite, King's Canyon, and Sequoia), three hours from San Francisco, three hours from the central coast, and four hours from Los Angeles! And, we had money. Real money! I remember my first monthly check as a professor was $2,300 (after taxes). I had never had a check that big! I never had a job with a four-digit monthly salary! We were rich!

By this time, Trina's parents had passed on, and my mother and father became Granny and Paw Paw for the entire family. We were a short drive from Mom and Dad. Our visits were often; our conversations were frequent.

Trina and I had reached that stage in life when your parents actually don't mind telling you how proud they are!

I was in my early thirties, a young husband, a fairly new father, a college professor, with a call to ministry. If ever there was a time I needed the wisdom of a *third-grade dropout,* it was then! I recall talks with my father that would last for hours. I was simply amazed by him. I knew all my life that he was a smart man, but I never realized how wise he was. When you're an absent-minded adolescent, a rebelling teen, or a know-it-all young adult, it's rather foreign to allow yourself energy to listen and be impacted by the wisdom of others. But now more than ever, I wanted to hear it all. I latched on to every word. I would ask him to repeat stories I had heard from childhood. I had the stories memorized. But now, I was searching for something different. For example, I knew there was always friction between my father and one of his superiors at the galley (cookhouse) at California Maritime Academy.

My father never complained, nor did he ever speak one bad word about the person in question. Yet, I just knew there was friction. I asked my father to recount story after story of how this supervisor made life miserable not just for my father but also for others who worked in the galley. Without disrespecting the person at all, my father would simply say, "Son, there will always be people in life who rub you the wrong way. Some you will work with, others you will work for. Make every effort to respect them. Make every effort to learn something from them. Son, sometimes you have to just stand. Sometimes you have to just hold firm—knowing that you will get through whatever it is."

Now I had heard this a million times, but I never got it. I never got it until I found myself in similar situations. The overwhelming tendency is to lash out, to defend yourself, to run, to flee. It is not natural to just *stand*.

Webster's Dictionary defines *stand* as "to remain in an upright position." An additional explanation defines the word more clearly as: "to maintain a specified position, attitude or course." For two decades, I have devoted my academic research to understanding the rhetorical dimensions of the civil rights movement during the twentieth century in America. When I think of the words, "maintain a specified position, attitude, or chosen path," I think of all those freedom fighters who never veered off course. They kept standing without regard to personal safety.

I think of Jackie Robinson, who on April 14, 1947, broke the color barrier in Major League Baseball. On one occasion, Robinson asked Brooklyn Dodger owner Wesley "Branch" Rickey, "Mr. Rickey do you want a man who has the courage to fight back?" Mr. Rickey replied, "Jackie, I want a man who has the courage not to fight back."

I think about Moses Wright, a Mississippi share-cropper, who stood alone in an all-white courtroom and identified the two men who killed his nephew, Emmett Till, in 1955.

I think about Joann Robinson, a worker for the Women's Political Council, who went into high gear following the December 1, 1955, arrest of Rosa Parks in Montgomery, Alabama. Robinson realized in order to start a boycott of the bus system, 50,000 blacks in Montgomery had to be notified within a 24-hour period—without the use of cell phones, fax machines, or e-mail messages. Robinson stood through the night mimeographing 35,000 leaflets, then she distributed them throughout the community. Because of Robinson, the one-day, December 5, 1955, bus boycott was so successful that organizations mounted an 11-month protest that resulted in the desegregation of Montgomery buses the following year. (For a thorough description and analysis of the boycott, please see David J. Garrow's *Bearing the Cross: Martin Luther King, Jr. and the Southern Christian Leadership Conference.* New York: Vintage Books, 1986.)

I think about those nine students who wanted to attend all-white Central High School in Little Rock, Arkansas, in 1957. It took great courage to stand—often against a mob of agitators.

I think of all the people who have stood in the face

of great danger. People such as Rev. Fred Shuttlesworth, whose home was bombed but whose heart remained strong. He kept standing.

Obviously I think of Martin Luther King, Jr., who received death threats every day of his life from 1955 until his eventual assassination April 4, 1968. In a speech the night before his death—a powerful oration known as "The Mountaintop Speech"—King makes clear his intention to stay the course—to keep standing regardless of what may occur:

> I don't know what will happen to me now. We've got some difficult days ahead. But it doesn't matter to me now because I have been to the mountaintop. I won't mind. Like anybody else, I would like to live a long life. Longevity has its place. But I'm not concerned about that now. I just want to do God's will. And He's allowed me to go to the mountaintop. And I've looked over, and I've seen the Promised Land. I may not get there with you, but I want you to know tonight that we as a people will get to the Promised Land. So I'm happy tonight. I am not worried about anybody. I am not fearing any man. "Mine eyes have seen the glory of. . . ."

So moved was King that he literally collapsed in the arms of supporters before finishing the line, "Mine eyes have seen the glory of the coming of the Lord." Regardless of the death threats, the body wracked with fatigue, the insurmountable pressures on him—he took one last opportunity to tell supporters, "I'm standing."

I'll show you standing. During the editing of this chapter—Dana Reeve, widow of actor Christopher Reeve, passed away from lung cancer. A non-smoker, Dana announced in 2005 that she had lung cancer; however, she continued to work through her and her late husband's foundation to bring more awareness to the plight of those who are paralyzed. Regardless of personal tragedy, regardless of personal illness, Dana Reeve kept standing to the very end. You talk about a hero. You talk about making an impact!

I wanted to hear every story my father could tell—especially stories about how he would make a choice to stand in the midst of adverse circumstances. I could not get enough of listening to my father. I hung to every word. I begged him to retell story after story—from getting burned in Seattle with boiling water while the training ship *Golden Bear* was in port and making a choice to work through pain, to learning to hold your head up with courage and confidence despite dodging arrows hurled by a climate of racism and intolerance toward people of color.

In my heart and in my mind, I am listening to the wisdom of a man who fought prejudice all his life by choosing to love people. I am listening to a man who stood and remained silent during the hurling of racial slurs. I am listening to a man tell me to never judge a person by the color of his or her skin, by the educational level, by the list of accomplishments. I'm listening to a man who had every reason to give up, yet he made a commitment to stand. To stand for his God. To stand for his family. To stand for that which was right—regardless of what people thought or said. I saw my father live this as a lifestyle—and now, I am listening to the wisdom—the nuggets of truth that supported every action.

You talk about a larger-than-life action hero! I'm listening intently and thinking to myself, "Rick, you've got to learn to just stand. Hang in there! Don't quit! Don't give up! Just stand!" I would never have imagined that in just a few months, I would have to stand on the wisdom of my father as never before.

Trina and I were quite pleased with the results from our annual physical exams and ready to take on 1991, a new year that was filled with promise and great expectation. Trina had retired from nursing by now and was pursuing a new career as librarian at our boys' Christian school—something that gave her immense pleasure. After years of intense hospital work, Trina found unspeakable joy and great satisfaction in teaching children to read and helping them develop a lifelong love affair with literature.

To this day, our older boys—both in college—are insatiable readers.

Despite the positive medical exam, Trina was worried about a lump she continued to feel in her left breast. The lump was not detected by a mammogram but through a self-exam. A week later, following a biopsy and more tests, Trina was told she had breast cancer. We did not realize the advanced stage of the disease until the mastectomy, which revealed the cancer had spread to the lymph nodes.

Our perfect dream world became a living nightmare. Days that were filled with joy and laughter were now clouded with tears and uncertainty. Weekends that were used to explore the diverse California landscape were now devoted to rest and recovery from surgery, chemotherapy, and radiation treatments. Constant doctor appointments and hospital visits robbed our family of any more spontaneity. Our sense of adventure was squelched with the hard reality that Trina had cancer—and things did not look good.

I put on the best spin in front of my family and friends. After all, I was a minister and "Mr. Positive." Inside, however, I wanted to run and hide. I could not help Trina. How would we make it? What would happen if she died? How would we go on? How would the boys make it?

I was a wreck and had very few people I could talk to. Allow me to make an important point here. I am a

Christian. I am a Christian minister. I love Christian people. However, Christians in general do a poor job responding to those who are suffering. Rather ironic, wouldn't you say? I knew all the appropriate verses. I knew the promises of God. I needed to be reassured with a hug, a handshake, a moment of your time to share a moment in silence. I needed to laugh, not cry. I needed to lift my head up, not have you cry on my shoulder to prove how deeply you ached. I quickly grew tired of Christians employing spiritual clichés. I needed something real to help me deal with the reality I was facing. I began reading my Bible like never before. And I began having long talks with my dad. I have to confess—*standing* was the last thing on my mind.

Nothing was omitted from our conversations. We discussed Trina's care and my response. We discussed the children's care and my response. We discussed subjects and scenarios that I did not want to discuss. I didn't realize it then, but this *third-grade dropout* was conducting a crash course in wisdom for his son. It was as if he'd been saving up all his life for such a time as this. He would not sit down and say, "Now son, you need to do this or that." Rather, he would let me talk, cry, even get mad. He would listen to me. He listened. He hurt. He ached. Trina was not just my wife. Trina was the daughter he never had. Trina was his heart—and the mother of his grandchildren. My father ached. But he kept teaching. He would say things like, "Son, now is the time to be a man. Your wife needs a man, not a boy. And I have not raised a boy. I have raised a man. And I am proud of you. And with God's help, you will make it through. And you begin right now by making a commitment—every day—to just stand."

My father spent his entire life standing. He stood against racial segregation in Texas. He stood in the wake of losing his father at an early age. He stood with dignity and taught his children to do the same regardless of education, class status, or economic level.

Now, needing to comfort a son with more than just clever wit, he was saying in his own way, "I've shown you how to be a man the best way I know how. Now you have to make a choice." It was during one of these conversations with my father—at my parents' house on Louisiana Street in Vallejo, California, I decided that no matter what, I was going to be a man. Trina needed a man of strength. Our sons needed visible assurance that everything was going to be alright. I needed to know beyond a shadow of a doubt that God would never leave my side. He never did.

My commitment to stand received the ultimate test a few years later. After six years of countless chemotherapy sessions and radiation treatments, my boys and I walked up to Mommy's casket and said goodbye. The worst day of my life was seeing my beloved Trina in a casket. Everything inside of me wanted to die. You are aware that people are watching you, but you no longer care. You just want to quit. You just want to give up. You want to go home—to heaven—so you can hold your wife again. I never knew the pain of a broken heart could hurt so deeply. I never knew loneliness so profound it could paralyze your life. I never knew a despondency that rendered me so desperate that I wanted to end my life. But the presence of my Heavenly Father held me up, while the tug of my two little fellows forced me to look up and the simple words of my father encouraged me to stand up. Right there at Trina's casket—September 11, 1996—I made a choice to stand.

A victorious decision to stand will always be met with resistance! The months following Trina's passing were filled with turmoil, confusion, bewilderment, loneliness, anger, frustration, resentment, and depression. I was on an emotional roller coaster with no end in sight. But during those months, and even to this day, I go back to the turning point in my life—the moment I decided to stand. I wish I could tell you it was my idea to just stand! That *third-grade dropout* had one last lesson he wanted to impart on his son.

My father was a big strapping Texan (6'2", 275 pounds) and afraid of nothing and nobody. He was a man's man and reared my brother and me to be the same. We were taught to respect others, never to look for trouble, but never to allow someone to run over us. I never saw my father shed a tear. The most emotional I had ever seen my father was at his mother's funeral a few years earlier, and the night Martin Luther King, Jr., was assassinated in Memphis, Tennessee—April 4, 1968. Though emotional, neither time did my father cry. However, at the conclusion of Trina's funeral, right before the funeral directors closed the lid of the casket for the last time, Daddy broke down. He composed himself, turned to me, put his arms on my shoulders and said some words I shall never forget. I don't recall most of what was said during Trina's funeral, but I remember what my father said word for word. First, whispering in my ear, he recited Ephesians 6:10, *Finally, my brethren, be strong in the Lord and in the power of His might.*[26] Next, he said the words that would change the course of my life:

Son, just stand!

Just stand. The best lesson I have ever received. The most profound lesson I have ever been taught. The best job training course I have ever taken. The best life coaching I have ever gained. The best—absolute best—advice I have ever received. My father's life was speaking to me. His life's experiences were telling me a story. It was a story that had two basic truths: 1) You can depend on God no matter what happens, and 2) If you can keep standing in the middle of hell, you will learn to walk again.

I was fortunate to have excellent teachers during my undergraduate years and master's training at California State University, Chico. I was blessed and challenged to encounter and interact with great thinkers during doctoral training at the University of Oregon. I count myself among the fortunate to have enjoyed outstanding colleagues in both the television industry and the various academic communities of which I have been privileged to be part. In all my fifty-plus years of living—including over twenty years obtaining an education—never have I received greater advice and more profound wisdom than the words whispered in my ear while standing at Trina's casket. Just stand! Just stand! "Son, just stand!"

Those simple yet profound words have carried me this last decade. A year later, I would have to stand again—this time over my father's casket. Then, just four years later, over my mother's casket. I am so grateful my father taught me one last lesson before he went home. As I look back, I now know that Dad strategically and methodically used the time of Trina's illness as my personal graduate school for life. He talked. I listened. Every one of his experiences—though they did not mirror my own—all featured the same qualities and characteristics:

> JUST STAND. THE BEST LESSON I HAVE EVER RECEIVED. THE MOST PROFOUND LESSON I HAVE EVER BEEN TAUGHT.

- Remain true to yourself.
- Think the best at all times.
- Give your best regardless of the circumstances.
- Keep standing no matter what.

From 1991 until his death in 1997, Roger Rigsby conducted a graduate seminar in leadership training. Class was confined to one student. Homework was tough and continues for a lifetime. You retake the class until you get it. And once you "get it," you continue taking the class and applying what you have learned for the rest of your life. You will receive your graduation diploma at a date yet to be determined.

My father spent his life preparing for a one-minute encounter at a casket. When he said, "just stand," I realized I had a choice to make. I must recommit to making that choice every day. As a result, I choose each day to be:

- Joyful
- Thankful
- Positive
- Victorious
- Honest
- Sincere
- Content

Let me make this clear. Life boils down to choices. You cannot choose what happens to you. You can choose how you will respond. I held on to Daddy's words. I can recall very specific times when they made the difference between life and death.

A month passed between Trina's funeral and when the reality began to set in that she was never coming back to Earth again. Such a reality is overwhelming to deal with and humanly impossible to accept. I recall visiting with my father and just listening to him tell me to stand. I remember making a choice to get up, move on, and get with it. Now, I would have to remind myself a hundred times a day about this choice. However, my father's wisdom to keep standing prevented me from quitting. His words to never give up caused me in some strange way to hope even in the face of hopelessness. It was as if Dad could see the sun through the clouds of despair.

As I continued listening to his words, I began to believe for myself that maybe, just maybe the boys and I could make it and we would be okay. I had to accept the hard fact that our lives would never be normal. I had to face the reality that people knew my business, and they made up what they did not know. When you grieve publicly, it's almost as if you become public property. But I also began embracing a new reality. We were survivors! We were alive! Our lives still had meaning and purpose!

Two years after gathering for Trina's home-going, we gathered at the same church for my marriage to Janet Sue Butcher! As crazy as this may sound, I honestly believe that Trina had a hand in selecting my darling Janet—a beautiful angel who is now the love of my life! Janet gave the boys and me space to grieve and a safe place to grow. Right after we were married, Janet adopted our older boys—thus fulfilling Trina's final request that her "babies not grow up without a mommy." A year after our marriage, our third son, Zachary, was born. Eighteen months later, our fourth son, Joshua, came into the world!

I am mindful that some who may be reading this have just lost a loved one—perhaps a spouse, maybe a child. As I tell my story all over the world, I am moved by the horrific accounts of men and women from all walks of life who share their personal stories of loss.

You might be going through a difficult valley right now. It may not be the loss of a loved one. It may be a difficult situation at work, a struggle in a marriage, or an impossible situation with a child. I have one word for you:

STAND!

Regardless of how you feel, you must continue standing. In fact, I had to learn that regardless of what you see, you must continue standing. Jonathan Swift said that vision is the ability to see the invisible.

I had to learn I could no longer trust my feelings and my emotions. They lied to me every day. I had to trust God. Had it not been for God, I would have given up. I would have committed suicide. I realize this may surprise you since I was a minister. The fact is when your spouse dies, you don't want to be here. And hearing people say things like, "Well, she's in a better place" does not help at all. Of course you are happy she is in a better place. But because you are hurting, you are allowing your emotions to dictate your condition. My emotions were purely selfish. If I couldn't have Trina on Earth, why would I want to remain?

VISION IS THE ABILITY TO SEE THE INVISIBLE.

So, I understand those who have no hope. I understand those who have no reason for which to hope. But I am evidence of a loving, caring, and merciful God. Try reaching out to Him—even if you don't believe He can help you. I was in the same boat. I did not think He could help me.

Then, I just made a decision that I could not cry month after month. So I called out, angrily at first. Frustrated, I had to work through a lot of emotions—and I probably will for the rest of my life. But I called out to God despite my feelings. And I did not like the answer!

Over and over, I heard the Creator of the universe—the One who could bring Trina back to us if He chose—say, "Rick, My son . . . can you trust Me?" This is not the response a hurting person wants to hear. But I also thought, "How ironic that my Heavenly Father is echoing what my earthly father said at Trina's casket. Will I trust God? Will I stand?"

This is about the most unspiritual thing I could say, but I figured I would stand . . . because I had nothing else to lose! What I did not realize then was that a small step of faith put an entire series of events in motion. I began reading the Bible like never before. I began to realize that nothing, absolutely nothing moved the hand of God except faith.

My dad was teaching me to have faith in God by telling me, "Son, just stand."

My father had been challenging me to stand for forty-five years. He modeled standing. He lived standing. And now he spoke standing.

Almost a year to the day after Trina passed away, Roger Marion Rigsby, age 77, went home to be with his Lord.

I will always be grateful for those last few days together. Although cancer was killing his body, his mind and heart were still intact. And even though he was leaving us slowly, the essence of my father was just as strong in that hospital bed as if he were standing on a podium.

"Dad, are you scared?"

"Heavens no, Son. God has blessed me with two wonderful sons, a wonderful wife, and an amazing life. And now I get to go home. You boys carry on. You carry on, Ricky. Carry on."

Even on his deathbed, he was teaching me to be a man. Especially on his deathbed, he was teaching me to be a man. Carry on. Stay the course. Hold your position. Keep standing.

Dad has always been right. "Son, if you can stand in the middle of great trouble, devastating circumstances, and unbearable pain, then you will walk again." For those who feel like giving up, I understand. But keep standing. The sun is about to shine. For those experiencing the excruciating pain of heartbreak, keep standing. Relief is on the way. For those who have no hope or reason for which to hope, keep standing. The longer you stand, the stronger you become! I have discovered that standing strengthens the heart and fortifies the will! Those who make a choice to stand will experience:

- Greater resourcefulness
- Reluctance to blame people or circumstances for difficult times

- Decreased desire to meet the expectation of others
- Greater joy
- Greater peace
- Greater passion for living

My dad was right. And now, he cannot hear me say, "Thank you." But in my own way I can say thanks to Roger Marion Rigsby. I can say thank you by:

- Being kind to others
- Being an hour early
- Helping people
- Doing a good job
- Living a life of integrity
- Always standing

What a great way to memorialize a great man. Dad, I promise to be kind to others. I can thank you by arriving early and staying late and helping anyone in need. I can say thank you by being a man of character and striving for excellence. I can say thank you for teaching me to stand when everything inside me wants to quit. Thank you, Dad, for imparting your profound wisdom into my life.

Everywhere I speak, a part of you is with me. Every book I write, your wisdom is reflected on the page. Every day of my life, I share your wisdom. Your words have become my words. As such, your wisdom lives on for a new generation to embrace.

Dad, I promise to keep loving, keep learning, and keep standing. I promise to share your simple words with everyone I meet. I promise to give my best to this, our wonderful country, just like you taught me. I promise to give my best to ministry, to speaking, to writing, to being a good person. Finally, I promise to give my best to my family, my friends, and most of all to my relationship with Christ.

Dad, thank you for being the greatest teacher any son could ever have.

Thank you, Daddy. Thank you for everything.

Always Standing.

NOTES

1. Jim Braham, "The Spiritual Side," *Industry Week,*
   February 1, 1999. http://www.industryweek.com
   /CurrentArticles/asp/ articles.asp?ArticleId=414.
   Retrieved April 5, 2006.
2. For more information about the Foundation, please visit
   www.actsofkindness.org.
3. Albert Einstein, "The World as I See It," originally
   published in *Forum and Century,* 84, pp. 193–194.
4. Abraham Maslow's Hierarchy of Needs appears in
   literature from a number of disciplines, including
   organizational communication, interpersonal
   communication, small group communication, as well
   as research in psychology and sociology. For a general
   overview of Maslow's discussion of human needs,
   review any basic text from the field of interpersonal
   communication. One example is Adler, Rosenfeld,
   and Proctor, *Interplay: The Process of Interpersonal
   Communication* (10th ed.), Oxford University Press, 2006.

5. Dr. Wayne W. Dyer, *The Power of Intention: Learning to Co-create Your World Your Way.* Carlsbad, California: Hay House, Inc., 2004, p. 25. This quote is part of an interesting discussion in Chapter Two titled "The Seven Faces of Intention."

6. David Van Biema, "A Defender of the Faith," *Time*, April 11, 2005, p. 39.

7. Roderick P. Hart, *Seducing America: How Television Charms the Modern Voter.* Thousand Oaks, California: Sage Publications, 1999.

8. Martin Lloyd-Jones, *Spiritual Depression.* Grand Rapids: Eerdmans Publishing Company, 1965.

9. Jay Dennis, Leading with *Billy Graham: The Leadership Principles and Life of T. W. Wilson.* Grand Rapids: Baker Books, 2005. Dennis does an outstanding job of culling specific principles from Wilson's life to demonstrate how living such a life gave him what Dennis refers to as next-level influence—a kind of influence that impacts generations.

10. Dorothy Leonard and Walter Swap, "Deep Smarts," *Harvard Business Review*, September 1, 2004.

11. Hal Himmelstein, *Television Myth and the American Mind.* Westport, CT: Praeger Publishers, 1984.

12. Eric Schlessor, *Fast Food Nation.* Houghton Mifflin, 2001.

13. David Maraniss, *When Pride Still Mattered: A Life of Vince Lombardi.* New York: Simon and Schuster, 1999, p. 30.

14. *USA Today*, 8/17/05. Article highlighted that a growing number of teachers are not returning to the classroom

after summer vacation and quoted one teacher, who described that it was becoming increasingly difficult to reach children.

15. John Mason, *An Enemy Called Average*. Tulsa, Oklahoma: Insight International, 1995. Mason simply and convincingly argues that the great problem in society is the absurd ambition to promote and proclaim average. He argues that such a mindset is stifling greatness and paralyzing excellence in American culture.

16. This quote appeared in an online publication compiled by the Maxwell Football Club, and featured contributions from Ray Didinger of NFL Films. To see the complete article, please go to http://www.maxwellfootballclub.org.

17. Stu Webber wrote an awesome book, *Four Pillars of a Man's Heart: Bringing Strength Into Balance* (Sisters, Oregon: Multnomah Books, 1997), in which he discusses the concept of "Playing the Man."

18. Joe Paterno, quoted in *USA Today*, November 19, 2005.

19. Malcolm Gladwell, *The Tipping Point: How Little Things Can Make a Big Difference*. New York: Bay Back Books, 2002, 9.

20. Dr. Howard G. Hendricks is a Distinguished Professor and Chairman of the Center for Christian Leadership at Dallas Theological Seminary. This quote is from his book, *A Life of Integrity*, 1997, Multnomah Publishers, Inc., Sisters, Oregon, p. 169.

21. General Chuck Yeager and Leo Janos, *Yeager*, 1985, New York: Bantam Books; pp. 252–253.

22. Dr. Rosberg shared this story November 20, 2005, during the national radio broadcast of "America's Family

Coaches Live," a call-in show which airs daily throughout the United States. The author was the special guest of hosts Dr. Gary Rosberg and his wife, Barbara.

23. Legendary college football coach R. C. Slocum was inducted into the Texas Sports Hall of Fame February 16, 2006, as part of the Class of 2005, which included Emmitt Smith (football), Tim Brown (football), Bela and Martha Karolyi (gymnastics), Zina Garrison (tennis), Augie Garrido (baseball), Bobby Bragan (baseball), and James Segrest (track and field). R. C. Slocum coached at Texas A&M for 31 years—14 as head football coach.

24. For an excellent discussion on how companies are being enhanced by the Sarbanes-Oxley Act, please review an article titled "The Unexpected Benefits of Sarbanes-Oxley" by Stephen Wagner and Lee Dittmar, *Harvard Business Review*, Vol. 84, Number 4, April 2006.

25. Mark Pyatt is the Director of Cross Industry Strategy and Solutions for SAP Labs, LLC. SAP is a Frankfurt, Germany based global business software solutions corporation and the leading business application software provider in the world with over 28,000 customers. The author wishes to thank Mr. Pyatt for granting numerous interviews about corporate business practices in general and the benefits of the Sarbanes-Oxley Act in particular.

26. *Ryrie Study Bible* (King James Version). Chicago: Moody Press, 1994.

ABOUT THE AUTHOR

In 2017, Dr. Rick Rigsby delivered one of the most passionate speeches ever heard. More than 200 million people worldwide have viewed the speech in a video that went viral in just a matter of days.

Dr. Rick Rigsby is President and CEO of Rick Rigsby Communications. The former award-winning journalist followed a television career with two decades as a college professor, most of those years at Texas A&M University, where he was named twice as an outstanding professor in the college of liberal arts. In addition to his teaching duties, Dr. Rick also served as character coach and chaplain for the Aggies football team.

The internationally acclaimed motivational speaker is a favorite among professional sports organizations, including the National Football League and the PGA. Dr. Rick's dynamic presentations motivate, empower, and inspire worldwide—from Africa, Asia, and Australia to the Americas, Europe, and Canada. Rick's audiences include *Fortune* 100 and *Fortune* 500 companies, academic communities, and service organizations. Dr. Rigsby is a frequent guest on numerous television and radio shows and a regular contributor on the Fox Business News Network.

Dr. Rigsby's landmark book, *Lessons from a Third Grade Dropout* is a *USA Today, Wall Street Journal,* and Amazon bestseller. His latest book, *Afraid to Hope,* is now available in markets worldwide.

For more information, visit www.rickrigsby.com.

Facebook: @DrRickRigsby

Instagram: DrRickRigsby

Twitter: @DrRickRigsby

Dr. Rigsby's viral video:

https://youtu.be/Bg_Q7KYWG1g